SPECTRUM
Test Practice
Grade 7

Published by

 Children's Publishing

Editors: Stephanie Oberc, Jerry Aten

 **Children's Publishing**

Published by McGraw-Hill Children's Publishing
Copyright ©2003 McGraw-Hill Children's Publishing

Send all inquiries to:
McGraw-Hill Children's Publishing
3195 Wilson Drive NW
Grand Rapids, Michigan 49544

Spectrum Test Practice—grade 7
ISBN: 1-57768-977-1

1 2 3 4 5 6 7 8 9 PHXBK 07 06 05 04 03 02

The McGraw-Hill Companies

Introduction 4
Letter to Parent/Guardian 7
Correlation to Standards 8

Reading
Vocabulary
Synonyms 11
Antonyms 12
Multi-Meaning Words 13
Words in Context...........................14
Sample Test: Vocabulary 15

Comprehension
Main Idea 17
Recalling Details 18
Inferencing 19
Fact and Opinion...........................20
Story Elements 21
Nonfiction 22
Fiction 28
Sample Test: Reading Comprehension..........34
Reading Practice Test: Answer Sheet............38
Reading Practice Test 39

Language
Mechanics
Punctuation 47
Capitalization and Punctuation 49
Sample Test: Language Mechanics 51

Language Expression
Usage...............................54
Sentences 57
Paragraphs 60
Sample Test: Language Expression..............63

Spelling 68
Sample Test: Spelling.......................70

Study Skills................................72
Sample Test: Study Skills.....................76
Language Practice Test: Answer Sheet 77
Language Practice Test...............................78

Math
Concepts
Numeration...............................88
Number Concepts.........................91
Fractions and Decimals 94
Sample Test: Concepts 97

Computation
Fractions 100
Decimals 102
Percents 104
Problem Solving...........................106
Sample Test: Computation 108

Applications
Geometry 111
Measurement 114
Problem Solving...........................116
Algebra...............................119
Sample Test: Applications 121
Math Practice Test: Answer Sheet 124
Math Practice Test...............................125

Science 131
Sample Test: Science.......................137
Science Practice Test: Answer Sheet 139
Science Practice Test...............................140

Social Studies 142
Sample Test: Social Studies.....................149
Social Studies Practice Test: Answer Sheet 151
Social Studies Practice Test.......................152

Answer Key 155

With increased accountability in ensuring academic success for all learners, testing now takes a significant amount of time for students in all settings. Standardized tests are designed to measure what students know. These tests are nationally normed. State tests are usually tied to specific academic standards identified for mastery.

For many students, testing can be a mystery. They fear not doing well and not knowing what to expect on the test. This *Spectrum Test Practice* book was developed to introduce students to both the format and the content they will encounter on tests. It was developed on the assumption that students have received prior instruction on the skills included. This book is designed to cover the content on a representative sample of state standards. The sampling of standards is found on pages 8–10, with a correlation to the skills covered in this book and a correlation to sample standardized tests. Spaces are provided to record the correlation to the tests being administered by the user of this book. Spaces are also provided to add standards that are specific to the user.

Features of *Spectrum Test Practice*

- Skill lessons, sample tests for subtopics, and comprehensive content area tests

- Clues for being successful with specific skills

- Correlation of skills to state standards and standardized tests

- Format and structure similar to other formal tests

- Written response required in the Science and Social Studies sections

- Reproducible for use by a teacher for a classroom

Overview

This book is developed within content areas (Reading, Language, Math, Science, and Social Studies). A comprehensive practice test follows at the end of the content area, with an answer sheet for students to record responses. Within each content area, specific subtopics have been identified. Sample tests are provided for each subtopic. Within each subtopic, specific skill lessons are presented. These specific skill lessons include an example and a clue for being successful with the skill.

Comprehensive Practice Test

A comprehensive practice test is provided for each content area. The subtopics for each area are identified below:

- **Reading**

    - Vocabulary (synonyms, antonyms, multi-meaning words, and words in context

    - Reading Comprehension (main idea, recalling details, sequencing, inferencing, drawing conclusions, fact and opinion, cause and effect, author's purpose, and story elements in fiction and nonfiction articles)

- **Language**

    - Language Mechanics (capitalization and punctuation)

    - Language Expression (usage, sentences, and paragraphs)

    - Spelling (both correct and incorrect spelling)

    - Study Skills (dictionary skills, reference materials, reading tables and graphs, book parts)

- **Math**
  - Concepts (numeration, number concepts, fractions and decimals)
  - Computation (operations with fractions, decimals, and percents)
  - Applications (algebra, geometry, measurement, and problem solving)
- **Science***
  - Plant/Animal Classification
  - Forms of Matter
  - Makeup of the Earth
  - Human Body
  - Astronomy
- **Social Studies***
  - The Americas
  - Europe
  - Ancient Civilizations
  - Economics
  - U.S. Government

*Since states and often districts determine units of study within Science and Social Studies, the content in this book may not be aligned with the content offered in all courses of study. The content within each area is grade level appropriate. It is based on a sampling of state standards. The tests in Science and Social Studies include both multiple choice and written answer.

Comprehensive Practice Test Includes

- Content Area (i.e. Language)
- Subtopics (i.e. Language Mechanics)
- Directions, examples, and test questions
- Separate answer sheet with "bubbles" to be filled in for answers

Sample Tests

Sample Tests are included for all subtopics. These sample tests are designed to apply the knowledge and experience from the skill lessons in a more formal format. No clues are included. These sample tests are shorter than the comprehensive tests and longer than the skill lessons. The skills on the test items are presented in the same order as introduced in the book.

Sample Tests Include

- Subtopic (i.e. Language Mechanics)
- Directions, examples, and test questions

Skill Lessons

Skill lessons include sample questions and clues for mastering the skill. The questions are formatted as they generally appear in tests, whether the tests are standardized and nationally normed or state specific.

Skill Lessons Include

- Subtopic (i.e. Language Mechanics)
- Skill (i.e. Punctuation)
- Directions and examples
- Clues for completing the activity
- Practice questions

Use

This book can be used in a variety of ways, depending on the needs of the students. Some examples follow:

- Review the skills correlation on pages 8–10. Record the skills tested in your state and/or district on the blanks provided.
- Administer the comprehensive practice test for each content area. Have students use the sample answer sheet in order to simulate the actual testing experience. The tests for Reading, Language, and Math are multiple

choice. Evaluate the results.

- Administer the sample test for the subtopics within the content area. Evaluate the results.

- Administer the specific skill lessons for those students needing additional practice with content. Evaluate the results.

- Use the skill lessons as independent work in centers, for homework, or as seatwork.

- Prepare an overhead transparency of skill lessons to be presented to a group of students. Use the transparency to model the skill and provide guided practice.

- Send home the Letter to Parent/Guardian found on page 7.

Clues for Getting Started

- Determine the structure for implementing *Spectrum Test Practice*. These questions may help guide you:

  - Do you want to assess the overall performance of your class in each academic area? If so, reproduce the practice test and sample answer sheet for each area. Use the results to determine subtopics that need additional instruction and/or practice.

  - Do you already have information about the overall achievement of your students within each academic area? Do you need more information about their achievement within subtopics, such as Vocabulary within Reading? If so, reproduce the sample tests for the subtopics.

  - Do your students need additional practice with some of the specific skills that they will encounter on the standardized test? Do you need to know which students have mastered

which skills? These skill lessons provide opportunities for instruction and practice.

- Go over the purpose of tests with your students. Describe the tests and the testing situation, explaining that the tests are often timed, that answers are recorded on a separate answer sheet, and that the questions cover material they have studied.

- Do some of the skill lessons together to help students develop strategies for selecting answers and for different types of questions. Use the "clues" for learning strategies for test taking.

- Make certain that students know how to mark a separate answer sheet. Use the practice test and answer sheet so that they are familiar with the process.

- Review the directions for each test. Identify key words that students must use to answer the questions. Do the sample test questions with the class.

- Remind students to answer each question, to budget their time so they can complete all the questions, and to apply strategies for determining answers.

Reduce the mystery of taking tests for your students. By using *Spectrum Test Practice*, you have the materials that show them what the tests will look like, what kinds of questions are on the tests, and ways to help them be more successful taking tests.

Note: The reading comprehension questions in all selections are in the same order: main idea, recalling details/sequencing, inferencing/drawing conclusions, fact and opinion/cause and effect; and story elements. This information can be used to diagnose areas for needed instruction.

Dear Parent/Guardian:

We will be giving tests to measure your child's learning. These tests include questions that relate to the information your child is learning in school. The tests may be standardized and used throughout the nation, or they may be specific to our state. Regardless of the test, the results are used to measure student achievement.

Many students do not test well even though they know the material. They may not test well because of test anxiety or the mystery of taking tests. What will the test look like? What will some of the questions be? What happens if I do not do well?

To help your child do his/her best on the tests, we will be using some practice tests. These tests help your child learn what the tests will look like, what some of the questions might be, and ways to learn to take tests. These practice tests will be included as part of your child's homework.

You can help your child with this important part of learning. Below are some suggestions:

- Ask your child if he/she has homework.
- Provide a quiet place to work.
- Go over the work with your child.
- Use a timer to help your child learn to manage his/her time when taking tests.
- Tell your child he/she is doing a good job.
- Remind him/her to use the clues that are included in the lessons.

If your child is having difficulty with the tests, these ideas may be helpful:

- Review the examples.
- Skip the difficult questions.
- Guess at those that you do not know.
- Answer all the questions.

By showing you are interested in how your child is doing, he/she will do even better in school. Enjoy this time with your child. Good luck with the practice tests.

Sincerely,

● **Grade 7**

Sample Standards

	Spectrum Test Practice Gr. 7	*CAT Level 71	**CTBS Level 71	Other	Other	Other
Reading						
Vocabulary						
Understanding Figurative Language	X	X	X			
Using Common Foreign Words			X			
Using Context Clues	X	X	X			
Using Synonyms and Antonyms	X	X	X			
Using Multi-Meaning Words	X		X			
Using Common Roots and Word Parts		X				
Other						
Comprehension						
Identifying Main Idea	X	X	X			
Using Graphic Organizers		X	X			
Comparing and Contrasting	X	X	X			
Reading Various Genre	X	X	X			
Summarizing	X	X	X			
Using Popular Media		X	X			
Identifying Author's Purpose		X	X			
Distinguishing Between Fact and Opinion	X	X				
Identifying Character Traits/Feelings		X	X			
Identifying Supporting Details	X	X	X			
Understanding Literary Devices		X	X			
Understanding Themes			X			
Drawing Conclusions	X	X	X			
Using Context Clues	X	X	X			
Analyzing Characterization		X	X			
Other						
Language						
Mechanics						
Expression						
Using Graphic Organizers		X	X			
Understanding Purpose		X	X			
Using Topic Sentences	X	X	X			
Using Supporting Sentences for Paragraphs	X	X	X			
Drawing Logical Conclusions	X	X	X			
Using Technology						
Using Editing Skills		X				
Using Different Types of Writing	X	X	X			
Using Simple, Compound, and Complex Sentences	X	X	X			
Using Proper Grammar	X	X	X			
Using Corrrect Capitalization and Punctuation	X	X	X			
Other						
Other						

* CAT 11 Terra Nova CAT™ ©2001 CTB/McGraw-Hill
** CTBS 11 Terra Nova CTBS® ©1997 CTB/McGraw-Hill

● Grade 7

Sample Standards	Spectrum Test Practice Gr. 7	*CAT Level 71	**CTBS Level 71	Other	Other	Other
Spelling						
Identifying Correct Spelling	X		X			
Identifying Incorrect Spelling	X		X			
Other						
Study Skills						
Using Reference Materials	X	X				
Other						
Math						
Concepts						
Numeration						
Comparing and Ordering Positive and Negative Integers	X					
Comparing and Ordering Fractions, Decimals, Percents	X					
Using Number Lines	X					
Using Scientific Notation and Square Roots	X	X				
Renaming Numbers	X					
Using Prime Factorization	X					
Recognizing Decimal-Fraction Equivalents	X					
Using Models	X	X				
Understanding Place Value	X	X	X			
Other						
Computation						
Using Operations on Positive and Negative Numbers	X	X	X			
Using Operations on Fractions, Decimals, Percents	X	X	X			
Using Rounding of Numbers	X					
Using Ratio and Proportion	X					
Calculating Percentages	X					
Using Estimation	X		X			
Using Mental Arithmetic						
Using Appropriate Operations	X	X	X			
Algebra and Functions						
Using Equations with Two Variables	X	X	X			
Using Formulas with Two Varibales	X	X	X			
Using Variables	X	X	X			
Using Graphs	X	X	X			
Other						
Geometry						
Understanding Coordinate Graphs	X	X	X			
Using the Pythagorean Theorem	X	X				
Using Transformations of Shapes	X	X				
Constructing 3-D Objects	X	X	X			
Finding/Comparing Area, Perimeter, and Volume	X	X	X			
Other						

 * CAT 11 Terra Nova CAT™   ©2001 CTB/McGraw-Hill
** CTBS 11 Terra Nova CTBS®   ©1997 CTB/McGraw-Hill

● Grade 7

Sample Standards	Spectrum Test Practice Gr. 7	*CAT Level 71	**CTBS Level 71	Other	Other	Other
Measurement						
Using Standard Units, Tools, and Scale to Measure	x	x	x			
Comparing Different Units of Measure	x	x				
Calculating Circumference	x					
Calculating Amounts of Money	x	x	x			
Other						
Data Analysis						
Probability						
Graphing Data	x	x				
Using Data to Predict Future Events		x	x			
Using Tree Diagrams						
Other						
Problem Solving						
Using Strategies to Solve Problems	x	x	x			
Estimating Results	x		x			
Recognizing Reasonable Solutions	x		x			
Identifying Relevant Information	x	x	x			
Other						
Science						
Understanding the Solar System	x	x	x			
Understanding the Earth	x	x	x			
Understanding the Sun	x	x	x			
Understanding Matter and Energy	x	x	x			
Understanding Food Webs		x	x			
Understanding the Basic Functions of Organisms	x	x	x			
Other						
Social Studies						
History						
Understanding Ancient Civilizations and Events	x	x				
Understanding the Interconnection of People	x	x	x			
Understanding the History of the Soutwest Pacific		x				
Understanding the Histories of Asia and Africa		x	x			
Other						
Government Economics						
Comparing Governments	x					
Understanding International Trade and Currencies						
Comparing Economic Issues	x	x	x			
Understanding Savings and Investments						
Using Gross Domestic Product for Comparing Standard of Living						
Geography						
Interepreting Maps		x	x			
Identifying the Major Regions and Cities in Asia, Africa, and the Southwest Pacific		x				

* CAT 11 Terra Nova CAT™ ©2001 CTB/McGraw-Hill
** CTBS 11 Terra Nova CTBS® ©1997 CTB/McGraw-Hill

READING: VOCABULARY

● **Lesson 1: Synonyms**

Directions: Read each item. Choose the answer that means the same or about the same as the underlined word.

Examples

A. make a <u>pledge</u>
- (A) profit
- (B) trip
- (C) promise
- (D) comment

B. <u>visualize</u> the scene
- (F) forget
- (G) enjoy
- (H) imagine
- (J) recall

 Clue If an answer is too difficult, skip it and move on to the next item. Come back to the skipped items later.

● **Practice**

1. <u>precise</u> measurement
   - (A) accurate
   - (B) incorrect
   - (C) approximate
   - (D) unnecessary

2. pleasant <u>encounter</u>
   - (F) entertainment
   - (G) meeting
   - (H) weather
   - (J) vacation

3. <u>reserve</u> a table
   - (A) clear
   - (B) save
   - (C) polish
   - (D) find

4. <u>preceded</u> the wedding
   - (F) after
   - (G) enjoying
   - (H) before
   - (J) attending

5. constant <u>interruption</u>
   - (A) attention
   - (B) thoughts
   - (C) intrusion
   - (D) motion

6. <u>invented</u> the automobile
   - (F) created
   - (G) preceded
   - (H) allowed
   - (J) initiated

7. recently <u>updated</u>
   - (A) joined
   - (B) modernized
   - (C) learned
   - (D) cloned

8. an <u>immediate</u> response
   - (F) unequaled
   - (G) unhurried
   - (H) instantaneous
   - (J) interesting

STOP

READING: VOCABULARY

● Lesson 2: Antonyms

Directions: Read each item. Choose the answer that means the opposite of the underlined word.

Examples

A. <u>cheerful</u> attitude
- (A) unhappy
- (B) joyful
- (C) indifferent
- (D) silent

B. <u>gentle</u> disposition
- (F) large
- (G) ungrateful
- (H) violent
- (J) breezy

 Clue If you are unsure if your answer is correct, make your best guess.

● Practice

1. <u>ancient</u> civilizations
   - (A) recent
   - (B) old
   - (C) immediate
   - (D) destroyed

2. <u>found</u> the handout
   - (F) established
   - (G) misplaced
   - (H) wrote
   - (J) invented

3. <u>omit</u> information
   - (A) include
   - (B) examine
   - (C) exclude
   - (D) find

4. <u>lush</u> jungle
   - (F) thick
   - (G) dark
   - (H) barren
   - (J) unexplored

5. <u>withheld</u> funds
   - (A) allowed
   - (B) updated
   - (C) adjusted
   - (D) contributed

6. <u>conceal</u> the answer
   - (F) reveal
   - (G) hide
   - (H) share
   - (J) discuss

7. <u>inert</u> ingredient
   - (A) added
   - (B) stirred
   - (C) flour
   - (D) active

8. <u>minimize</u> problems
   - (F) increase
   - (G) decrease
   - (H) challenging
   - (J) word

STOP

READING: VOCABULARY

● Lesson 3: Multi-Meaning Words

Directions: Read each item. Choose the correct meaning for each underlined word.

Examples

A. The <u>passage</u> appeared in the magazine.
- (A) exit
- (B) crossing
- (C) journey
- (D) quotation

B. I <u>introduced</u> my dad to my teacher.
- (F) proposed
- (G) familiarized
- (H) submitted
- (J) suggested

Clue If you are not sure which answer is correct, take your best guess. Eliminate answer choices you know are wrong.

● Practice

1. The boat pulled up to the <u>landing</u>.
- (A) touching down
- (B) a dock
- (C) the level part of a staircase
- (D) taking off

2. The horses were <u>sheltered</u> in the barn.
- (F) housed
- (G) shielded
- (H) concealed
- (J) exposed

3. Karyn <u>registered</u> for the computer class.
- (A) listed
- (B) enlisted
- (C) enrolled
- (D) noticed

4. The poet led a <u>colorful</u> life.
- (F) bright
- (G) brilliant
- (H) distinctive or unique
- (J) multicolored

5. The deer was hidden in a <u>stand</u> of trees.
- (A) a small retail business
- (B) a raised platform
- (C) holding a position
- (D) a group of plants

6. Facts about antelopes were found in this <u>obscure</u> book.
- (F) hide
- (G) little-known
- (H) baffling
- (J) mysterious

7. The company <u>recalled</u> the cars because of safety concerns.
- (A) repealed
- (B) remembered
- (C) reinstated
- (D) summoned

STOP

READING: VOCABULARY

● **Lesson 4: Words in Context**

Directions: Read the sentences. Find the word that fits each blank the best.

Examples

A. Do not set your tent up on a
_____.

- Ⓐ hump
- Ⓑ overlook
- Ⓒ grassland
- Ⓓ beach

B. It would not _____ a good night
of sleep.

- Ⓕ change
- Ⓖ characterize
- Ⓗ facilitate
- Ⓙ hinder

 Clue Look for clue words in each sentence that can help you figure
out the correct answers.

● **Practice**

1. Could the energy from the ocean be
used to _____ electricity?

- Ⓐ conduct
- Ⓑ generate
- Ⓒ flow
- Ⓓ capture

2. Earth's forces that _____ together
will some day change coal into diamonds.

- Ⓕ crash
- Ⓖ collide
- Ⓗ join
- Ⓙ compress

3. A large meteor hitting the earth could
_____ a canyon.

- Ⓐ gouge
- Ⓑ touch
- Ⓒ encompass
- Ⓓ divide

4. Many years of action of rain and wind
will _____ the surface of a hill.

- Ⓕ enlarge
- Ⓖ plane
- Ⓗ alter
- Ⓙ correct

5. A large earthquake will cause the
ground to crack and _____.

- Ⓐ float
- Ⓑ rupture
- Ⓒ rotate
- Ⓓ melt

6. People can die from the _____ in
the air after a volcano erupts.

- Ⓕ ash
- Ⓖ moisture
- Ⓗ rain
- Ⓙ oxygen

STOP

READING: VOCABULARY
SAMPLE TEST

● **Directions:** Read each item. Choose the answer that means the same or about the same as the underlined word.

Examples

A. The <u>village</u> has only one school.
- (A) city
- (B) district
- (C) country
- (D) hamlet

B. When the employee stole money, he was <u>corrupt</u>.
- (F) dishonest
- (G) truthful
- (H) helpful
- (J) prosecuted

For numbers 1–2, read each item. Choose the answer that means the same or about the same as the underlined word.

1. Nick <u>insisted</u> that his friend read the book.
- (A) regarded
- (B) answer
- (C) pretended
- (D) urged

2. <u>Individuals</u> within the group had <u>different</u> points of view.
- (F) enabled
- (G) similar
- (H) varied
- (J) controlled

For numbers 3–6, read each item. Choose the answer that means the opposite of the underlined word.

3. That chemical is <u>volatile</u>!
- (A) stable
- (B) explosive
- (C) useful
- (D) puzzling

4. Joshua was filled with <u>sorrow</u> when his dog died.
- (F) danger
- (G) joy
- (H) passion
- (J) anger

5. How many answers were <u>correct</u>?
- (A) wrong
- (B) right
- (C) difficult
- (D) justified

6. It is <u>questionable</u> if it will rain on Saturday.
- (F) doubtful
- (G) uncertain
- (H) inevitable
- (J) possible

GO ON

READING: VOCABULARY
SAMPLE TEST (cont.)

For numbers 7–10, choose the correct meaning for the underlined word.

7. **When we eat, we digest food.**
    - (A) journal
    - (B) absorb
    - (C) inhale
    - (D) chew

8. **Look at the picture on the computer monitor.**
    - (F) album
    - (G) supervisor
    - (H) system
    - (J) screen

9. **Keep a diary of your daily activities.**
    - (A) autobiography
    - (B) record
    - (C) periodical
    - (D) index

10. **That word adds punch to your sentence!**
    - (F) pungency
    - (G) drinks
    - (H) nothing
    - (J) power

For numbers 11–14, find the word that fits each blank the best.

11. **We stayed at a _____ hotel, and we took a beach walk each day.**
    - (A) seaside
    - (B) mountain
    - (C) resort
    - (D) cheap

12. **We got lost because we traveled a _____ way.**
    - (F) long
    - (G) slow
    - (H) special
    - (J) roundabout

13. **He is so _____ that people enjoy spending time with him.**
    - (A) boring
    - (B) unfriendly
    - (C) congenial
    - (D) unhappy

14. **The energy from the sun is _____ because it never stops shining.**
    - (F) hot
    - (G) constant
    - (H) dying
    - (J) warm

STOP

READING: READING COMPREHENSION

● **Lesson 5: Main Idea**

Directions: Read each item. Choose the sentence that best answers each question.

Example

Newspapers serve as resources for students doing research, shoppers searching for bargains, and voters making decisions about candidates. Not everything you read in a newspaper is factual, though. Sometimes feature articles can contain opinions, and sometimes advertisements can contain facts.

A. **What is the main idea of this paragraph?**

  (A) Newspapers can be a source of factual information.

  (B) You can find a lot of good information in newspapers.

  (C) Students should use newspapers when doing research.

  (D) Newspapers are filled with lies.

 Skim the passage then read the questions. Refer back to the passage to find the answers. You don't have to reread the story for each question.

● **Practice**

Strange, But True

Frivolous lawsuits have repeatedly been in the news. The family of Giovanni A. Almovodar, New Jersey prison inmate, filed a lawsuit against the Camden County jail. The inmate was 18 and awaiting trial on a murder charge. He died when he fell on his head during an escape attempt. The family charged that the jailers did not maintain a "reasonably safe facility."

In Davis, California, a 31-year-old woman successfully sued City Hall for stress, humiliation, and lost wages when her neighbor complained about her snoring. A noise enforcement officer fined the snoring woman $50, but the case against her was dropped. However, she felt the embarrassment was worth $24,500. She took City Hall to court, and eventually settled the case for $13,500.

Yes, truth is definitely much stranger than fiction. But, that is what makes this world such an interesting place!

1. **Which sentence best describes the main idea of this story?**

  (A) Lawsuits cost the public hundreds of thousands of dollars each year.

  (B) It is amazing what some people will take to court.

  (C) Most people do not sue for unreasonable things.

  (D) Don't let your neighbor hear you snore.

2. **Which of the following titles would also be appropriate for this passage?**

  (F) "Crazy People"

  (G) "Family Blames Death on Facility"

  (H) "Snoring Brings Profits"

  (J) "Unreasonable Lawsuits"

READING: READING COMPREHENSION

● Lesson 6: Recalling Details

Directions: Read each item. Choose the item that best answers each question.

Example

Before he could react, the car door slammed, the motor gunned, and Barrett was jerked over the ridge and down the front side of the roof. He landed on the lawn at the front of the house. His leg was broken, but Barrett's friend reported that the man was lucky to be alive.

A. Who was injured?

- (A) Barrett
- (B) a man
- (C) Barrett's friend
- (D) the reporter

 Clue Read the story carefully and try to remember the details.

● Practice

Alex in Charge

Alex was thrilled. Finally she was allowed to babysit her sister Connie by herself. Connie was four. When their parents left, Alex and Connie sat down to watch TV. "We're watching my show because I'm in charge," said Alex. Connie burst into tears, stood right in front of the TV, and wouldn't move. "Fine. Then let's eat. But we're eating what I want because I am in charge."

Alex microwaved the leftover macaroni and cheese and gave some to Connie. Connie turned the bowl upside down. "You did that on purpose!" said Alex. "You are going to bed right now because I am in charge!" She carried a screaming Connie to the bedroom.

All of a sudden, Connie stopped crying. "What's that?" she said in a small, frightened voice. Alex listened and heard a strange noise. It sounded as if someone was climbing up the side of the house! Just then a huge, dark shadow fell across the room. Alex and Connie both screamed and held onto each other. They crept to the window in silence. They peered over the windowsill and saw a tree scratching against the pane. Sighing with relief, they both fell exhausted onto Connie's bed and went to sleep.

1. How old was Connie?

- (A) three
- (B) four
- (C) five
- (D) the story does not say

2. Where did the girls' parents go?

- (F) to the movies
- (G) to dinner
- (H) to buy a microwave
- (J) The story does not say.

 STOP

READING: READING COMPREHENSION

● Lesson 7: Inferencing

Directions: Read each item. Choose the sentence that best answers each question.

Example

Michael Jordan wasn't born a star. He did have natural talent, but his success was a result of his family's support and these two qualities: hard work to overcome obstacles, and turning defeat into a challenge!

A. **Which of the following is probably true about Michael Jordan?**

- (A) He would quit when he was defeated.
- (B) He never got enough rest.
- (C) He did not give up when things were difficult.
- (D) He liked to eat ice cream.

Read the passage. Then read the questions. Refer back to the passage to help you answer the questions. You don't have to reread the story for each question.

● Practice

Tanning Debate

The medical profession knows there is no such thing as a "healthy" tan. A tan is evidence of skin damage. Exposure to the sun causes the breakdown of collagen and elastic tissue in the skin. This in turn causes cosmetic problems such as wrinkles, freckles, and broken capillaries. But the most serious result of exposure to the sun is the increased risk of skin cancer.

No sunscreen can offer 100 percent protection. There are additional precautions a person must take in order to be completely safe from the damaging effects of the sun's rays. First of all, avoid the sun when it is strongest, from 10:00 A.M. until 2:00 P.M. When in the sun, wear a hat with a brim to protect the face and neck. Sunglasses protect the eyes from UV rays, and sunscreen can protect especially sensitive areas like the ears, forehead, nose, cheeks, and lips. Finally, wear protective clothing.

1. **What can you conclude from the story?**

- (A) Avoid the sun at all times.
- (B) Everyone who gets too much sun exposure gets skin cancer.
- (C) You will never age if you avoid the sun.
- (D) Limiting sun exposure can lead to a healthier life.

2. **Which of the following can be the result of too much exposure to the sun?**

- (F) premature aging of the skin
- (G) fainting spells at the beach
- (H) becoming tired
- (J) a healthy tan

STOP

Name _____ Date_____

● **Lesson 8: Fact and Opinion**

Directions: Read each item. Choose the sentence or phrase that answers each question.

Example

Archaeologists study the ruins of historical buildings. Some of the buildings are many thousands of years old. I think we can learn much about our past from their work.

A. **Which phrase from the paragraph gives us a clue that some of the content is opinion?**

- (A) our past
- (B) from their work
- (C) Some of the buildings
- (D) I think

 Clue You don't have to reread the story for each question.

● **Practice**

Leadbelly's Legacy

When you play your favorite rock or rap CD, you probably don't realize that you are enjoying the legacy of "Leadbelly." Born in 1888, Huddie Ledbetter, nicknamed "Leadbelly," was a blues guitarist who inspired generations of musicians.

For much of Huddie Ledbetter's life, he wandered from place to place, playing anywhere he could. In 1934, he was discovered by John and Alan Lomax, who helped him find a larger audience for his music. Soon he was playing in colleges, clubs, and music halls. He was featured on radio and television shows.

Leadbelly died in 1949, but his music lives on. Musicians in every style credit him with laying the foundation for today's popular music. From rock and roll to rap, American music owes a great debt to Leadbelly.

1. **Which of the following sentences is a fact?**
   - (A) Everyone loves Leadbelly.
   - (B) In 1934, he was discovered by John and Alan Lomax.
   - (C) American music owes a great debt to Leadbelly.
   - (D) Leadbelly liked playing at clubs the most.

2. **A fact—**
   - (F) cannot be proven true or false.
   - (G) can be proven true or false.
   - (H) cannot be tested.
   - (J) is a theory.

 STOP

READING: READING COMPREHENSION

● Lesson 9: Story Elements

Directions: Read each item. Choose the best sentence or phrase to answer each question.

Example

When they got to the theme park, nobody told the teachers about the coaster challenge. The kids in the challenge forged ahead to the first coaster—The Reptile. It snaked around a large area.

A. **This paragraph could be the first in a story about—**

- (A) a contest between some of the students.
- (B) teachers being afraid to ride roller coasters.
- (C) The Reptile.
- (D) a water park.

Skim the passage then read the questions. Refer back to the passage to find the answers. You don't have to reread the story for each question.

● Practice

Visiting Aunt Rita

My name is Lorenzo, and I want to tell you about a place I like. Aunt Rita lives in an adobe house in a small New Mexico town.

A couple of times a year, we drive to Aunt Rita's for a long weekend. I get to invite my best friend, Maggie. It takes a whole day to drive there.

There are always some chores to do during our visit. However, they are different from the ones I do at home, so I don't mind doing them. My assignment is to help in the garden. Depending on the season, we either plant, maintain, or harvest vegetables.

In the evening we prepare our meal. My favorite dinner is vegetable soup with fresh tortillas or bread. We always eat around an old wooden table. We talk about our day and make plans for the next day. Time goes by quickly when we stay with Aunt Rita because we do many things that we don't get to do at home.

1. **Which of the following is true about Lorenzo?**

- (A) Lorenzo is selfish.
- (B) Lorenzo does not have very many friends.
- (C) Lorenzo likes to eat chicken soup.
- (D) Lorenzo is a helpful person.

2. **What is one reason why Lorenzo's family visits his Aunt Rita a couple of times each year?**

- (F) They like to make vegetable soup.
- (G) The vegetable garden needs to be maintained throughout the year.
- (H) Because Maggie likes to go for the visit.
- (J) Lorenzo likes to invite Maggie.

READING: READING COMPREHENSION

● Lesson 10: Nonfiction

Directions: Read each item. Choose the best answer for each question.

Example

Historians point out that tattoos have been around for a long time. Egyptian tombs pictured tattooed people, showing that the practice dates back at least to 12,000 B.C. The practice spread to China and Japan and into Europe.

A. **The practice of tattooing dates back at least how many years from today?**

- (A) 14,000
- (B) 12,000
- (C) 10,000
- (D) There is not enough information to tell.

Skim the passage then read the questions. Refer back to the passage to find the answers. You don't have to reread the story for each question.

● Practice

Hunting the Causes of Lightning

More than 200 years after Benjamin Franklin flew a kite into a lightning storm, scientists still are not certain what causes lightning. Studies conducted on spring nights over the skies of the Great Plains states may help scientists find the causes. On spring nights, cool air converges with warmer air, triggering the storms that produce lightning.

One theory states that a bigger bit of ice slams into a smaller bit of ice, leaving behind a positive or negative charge. The larger the bit of ice and the faster it is going, the bigger the charge it leaves behind. When enough of these charges collect, lightning occurs. Scientists with the National Oceanic and Atmospheric Administration measure the size of the particles, their speed, wind speed, temperature, and air pressure, looking for the combination that tends to produce lightning.

In the spring of 1998, scientists uncovered another clue that may help unravel the causes of lightning. That spring, smoke from massive Mexican fires drifted over the south-central United States. Texas, Oklahoma, Colorado, and Nebraska were most affected. In those same areas, a strange phenomenon was noted. Between 60 and 70 percent of the lightning strikes proved to be positively charged. Usually, about 90 percent of lightning strikes are negatively charged.

Why is it important to know what causes lightning? Lightning causes fires and electrical damage, especially positively charged lightning such as that noted in the spring of 1998. Lightning is the number one storm-related killer in the United States. Statistics compiled by the National Weather Service indicate that each year more people are killed by lightning than by tornadoes and hurricanes combined. The first step in preventing those deaths is to understand what produces lightning.

GO ON

READING: READING COMPREHENSION

● Lesson 10: Nonfiction (cont.)

1. **What is the main idea of the story?**
   - Ⓐ Damage and deaths due to lightning might be able to be prevented.
   - Ⓑ We will never understand lightning.
   - Ⓒ Lightning does a lot of damage.
   - Ⓓ Scientists are conducting research in Texas.

2. **With which organization are scientists doing research on lightning causes?**
   - Ⓕ National Oceanic and Atomic Administration
   - Ⓖ National Oceanic and Atmospheric Administration
   - Ⓗ National Weather Service
   - Ⓙ National Atmospheric and Oceanic Administration

3. **What can you conclude after reading the story?**
   - Ⓐ The study of lightning is uninteresting to many people.
   - Ⓑ There is less lightning now than 60 years ago.
   - Ⓒ We know all we need to about lightning.
   - Ⓓ Scientists will continue to study lightning.

4. **Based on the information in the story, which is an opinion about lightning?**
   - Ⓕ Usually, 90 percent of lightning strikes are negatively charged.
   - Ⓖ Lightning causes fires and electrical damage.
   - Ⓗ Lightning causes deaths each year.
   - Ⓙ Scientists are searching for the cause of lightning.

5. **What causes lightning?**
   - Ⓐ Summer storms cause lightning.
   - Ⓑ Bits of ice bump together to create positive and negative charges.
   - Ⓒ Hot and warm air converging together causes lightning.
   - Ⓓ Lightning is caused by tornadoes.

6. **In what year did scientists unravel a special clue?**
   - Ⓕ 1998
   - Ⓖ 1987
   - Ⓗ 1988
   - Ⓙ 1989

STOP

Name _____ Date_____

● **Lesson 11: Nonfiction**

Directions: Read each item. Choose the best answer for each question.

Examples

Most people know that Jackie Robinson was the first African American to play on a major league baseball team. They "know" wrong. Moses Fleetwood "Fleet" Walker holds that honor. Walker was a catcher for the Toledo Blue Stockings, a team that joined the fledgling major league American Association in 1884.

A. **Based on the information in the paragraph, Robinson and Walker were—**

(A) the first two African-American major league baseball players.

(B) good friends.

(C) the best players on their teams.

(D) on the same team but at different times.

 Skim the passage then read the questions. Refer back to the passage to find the answers. You don't have to reread the story for each question.

● **Practice**

Croon a Tune

Scientists have long known that children's language skills may never catch up if their first babbled words are ignored. Some say that the same phenomenon may happen if budding musical talent is not reinforced. For example, few professional violinists begin serious study later than age seven or eight. A study at Beth Israel Deaconess Medical Center in Boston discovered that some classical musicians' brains were measurably larger than those of people who had not studied music. Gottfried Schlaug of Germany also found differences in the brains of people who began studying music early in life. Michael Phelps of UCLA found that when a trained musician listens to music, one area of the brain is most active. When a nonmusician listens, another area is most active.

An infant may be as driven to create and appreciate music as she is to understand language. Norman M. Weinberger, a psychobiologist who studies the link between behavior and biology, points out three signs that music listeners may be responding to a biological cue. One sign is that all cultures have music. Also, a behavior with biological roots might show up in infancy. Your young charge's song might not have won her any awards at a talent contest, but research confirms that by 11 months of age, infants can distinguish melodies. They can also detect changes in rhythm.

Recent advances in brain imaging point out a third evidence of the biological basis of music.

READING: READING COMPREHENSION

● Lesson 11: Nonfiction (cont.)

Using PET scans, scientists study how the brain responds to music. Most language functions are controlled by an area in the left half of the brain. Listening to melodies, the part of a song we hum, produced brain activity in the same area. Other elements of musical interpretation turned out to be controlled by different areas of the brain.

The next time you are babysitting and an infant croons a song to you, croon it right back to her. You may be helping to develop another classical musician or theoretical mathematician.

1. **Which of the following could be another good title for this story?**
   - (A) Music Plays Important Role in Language Development
   - (B) Music Plays Important Role in Learning Songs
   - (C) Sing-a-Long with Baby
   - (D) The Link Between Music and Brain Development

2. **People can distinguish melodies by which age?**
   - (F) 11 years
   - (G) 7 years
   - (H) 8 months
   - (J) 11 months

3. **Which of the following skills would music probably not help develop?**
   - (A) learning to wash dishes
   - (B) learning to dance
   - (C) learning about science
   - (D) learning another language

4. **Based on the information in the story, which of the following is not true?**
   - (F) Infants can detect changes in rhythm.
   - (G) Music can help develop math skills.
   - (H) Early exposure to music will definitely make you a musician.
   - (J) There are differences in the brains of musicians who studied music early in life.

5. **Which of the following is not a way in which language and music development are similar?**
   - (A) All cultures have both language and music.
   - (B) Both produce activity in the right side of the brain.
   - (C) Both produce activity in the left side of the brain.
   - (D) Both music and language seem to have biological roots.

6. **Who found differences in the brains of people who began studying music early in life?**
   - (F) Gottfried Schlaug
   - (G) Norman M. Weinberger
   - (H) Michael Phelps
   - (J) Wolfgang Amadeus Mozart

READING: READING COMPREHENSION

● **Lesson 12: Nonfiction**

Directions: Read each item. Choose the best answer for each question.

Example

Viruses cause colds. They cause more serious diseases, too, such as meningitis, an inflammation of the brain. Doctors have few medications to use against viruses since antibiotics do not help with viral illness. Antibiotics kill bacteria, but do not affect viruses.

A. **Antibiotics will help kill which of the following?**

(A) meningitis

(B) a bacterial infection

(C) the common cold

(D) acquired immune deficiency syndrome (AIDS)

 Clue Skim the passage then read the questions. Refer back to the passage to find the answers. You don't have to reread the story for each question.

● **Practice**

Mummies Have No Secrets

Mummies cannot hide their age. They cannot hide what they ate for their last meals or whether their families were wealthy or poor. Mummies cannot hide much of anything from anthropologists.

Wrappings and artifacts reveal much about the social status of the person while alive. For example, a mummy found in the Taklimakan Desert sported a bronze earring and leather boots. The decorations on these items showed that his people were skilled artisans.

A mummy's body reveals even more clues than its wrappings. The contents of a mummy's digestive tract can be examined chemically and microscopically, giving anthropologists clues about the person's diet. When anthropologist studied the Iceman, a mummy found in Italy, they examined the contents of his intestines. They wanted to see what he ate in the hours before his death. Organs and bones reveal

details about the way the person died, too. Even if no flesh remains, bones and teeth might reveal the age of the person at death, as well as some details about diet, height, occupation, ethnicity, and social status. A male mummy's worn front teeth might indicate that he used his teeth to hold a tool, freeing his hands for other work. In addition, since bone absorbs minerals during a person's life, a chemical study of the bones turns up information about the diet of the deceased person. If DNA can be extracted from a mummy, scientists can even determine the blood type of the deceased person.

Even death and 5,000 years cannot hide a mummy's secrets. These secrets are contributing to what we know about ancient life.

 GO ON

READING: READING COMPREHENSION

● Lesson 10: Nonfiction (cont.)

1. **What is the main idea of the passage?**
   - (A) Modern science can help us learn about ancient human life.
   - (B) Ancient people ate the same things we did.
   - (C) People used to dress very differently than we do.
   - (D) Anthropologists studied the Iceman.

2. **A mummy found in which desert wore a gold earring?**
   - (F) Tulsa Desert
   - (G) Taklimakan Desert
   - (H) Egyptian Desert
   - (J) Sahara Desert

3. **Scientific testing may allow us to know all but which one of the following?**
   - (A) We may know if the person had a disease.
   - (B) We may know exactly how old the person was when they died.
   - (C) We may know if the person enjoyed listening to music.
   - (D) We may know if the person took a medicine.

4. **Which sentence below is not a fact based on the passage?**
   - (F) A mummy's digestive tract can be examined.
   - (G) Wrappings and artifacts reveal much about the mummy's life.
   - (H) Scientists believe that mummies can be cloned with DNA.
   - (J) The Iceman was found in Italy.

5. **If the following sentences were placed in order, which one would be number two?**
   - (A) A chemical reaction helps determine what the mummy ate.
   - (B) The digestive tract is examined with chemicals.
   - (C) A mummy is found in the Taklimakan Desert.
   - (D) The mummy is taken to a research facility.

6. **Which of the following would not give us a clue as to the mummy's social status?**
   - (F) food
   - (G) clothes
   - (H) jewelry
   - (J) height

STOP

READING: READING COMPREHENSION

● Lesson 13: Fiction

Directions: Read each item. Choose the best answer for each question.

Example

The first dance of the year for the new seventh-graders was coming quickly. They had been waiting for this since school had begun. There would be decorations, snacks, and even a disc jockey to play music. The girls were talking about what they would wear.

A. **Which of the following will not be a part of the dance?**

- (A) dinner
- (B) snacks
- (C) decorations
- (D) disc jockey

 Skim the passage then read the questions. Refer back to the passage to find the answers. You don't have to reread the story for each question.

● Practice

Medieval Madness

"This is one reason I couldn't wait to be in the seventh grade," said Maribel enthusiastically. "Medieval Madness! We get to dress up in long, flowing dresses with veils and tall hats. The boys treat us like damsels in distress and do daring things for us. The jousting! The food! The party! I can barely stand it, I'm so excited!" With that, Maribel practiced a low curtsy.

"You girls always like this stuff," scoffed Daniel. "You sit around in those dumb dresses and dunce caps with veils while we go out to slay the dragons, so to speak. I do like the jousting part, though. I wish they'd let us use real lances. Those medieval guys had some bad weapons. Crossbows, mace, lances, and other kinds that have long disappeared. Too bad you girls just sit around and curtsy and wait for us to come back from doing the important jobs."

"Don't forget that men died in battle, people were tortured and enslaved, diseases were abundant, and not everyone was a knight or a lady. Ordinary people led miserable lives. They were often taxed to death, according to my mother. They had little to eat, and they never knew when their country would be invaded," Bo said.

"You're not going to spoil it for me," said Linnette. "I'm not saying I'd like to live in those days, but I'm glad we're having Medieval Madness. I'm going to be Guinevere for a day. Then at night, I'll go home, sit on my sofa, snack on some popcorn, and watch a video. I bet the real Guinevere would have liked that a lot!"

 GO ON

READING: READING COMPREHENSION

● Lesson 13: Fiction (cont.)

"Well, I think I'll be Merlin," said Bo. "He had the real power. I wish he really existed and could come to my house. I'd show him power that would knock his socks off. He'd declare me the real sorcerer as I sit in a chair and zap the TV on with the remote, turn on lights with a switch, cook in a microwave, and write on my computer!"

1. Which of the following is the main idea of the story?

- (A) Medieval times are fun to act out, but might not be fun to live in.
- (B) Merlin was the man with power.
- (C) We don't know if Merlin really existed.
- (D) Jousting and fighting were common.

2. What did Maribel practice?

- (F) making dresses
- (G) cooking
- (H) jousting
- (J) curtsying

3. What is probably true about living in medieval times?

- (A) Medicines were available.
- (B) Life was very difficult for many people.
- (C) Women had the same rights as today.
- (D) Food was plentiful for most people.

4. Which of the following is an opinion based on the information in the story?

- (F) Life was difficult for many people in medieval times.
- (G) Men died in battle in medieval times.
- (H) Daniel is in the seventh grade.
- (J) Guinevere would have liked popcorn.

5. What did Merlin have?

- (A) popcorn
- (B) videos
- (C) power
- (D) lance

6. In medieval days people endured all but which one of the following hardships?

- (F) starvation
- (G) taxes
- (H) invasions
- (J) computer crashes

STOP

READING: READING COMPREHENSION

● Lesson 14: Fiction

Directions: Read each item. Choose the best answer for each question.

Example

The new girl sat at the back of the room in science class. Emily, Linnette, Maribel, and the other girls were always interested in a new friend, but this girl seemed to really keep to herself. She sat in the back with her feet up on the empty seat next to her.

A. **What is the new girl's name?**
- (A) The passage does not tell us.
- (B) Emily
- (C) Linnette
- (D) Maribel

 Clue Skim the passage then read the questions. Refer back to the passage to find the answers. You don't have to reread the story for each question.

● Practice

In the Frigid Wilderness

That grueling night lingered on and on. I was not a stranger to the below-zero temperatures, the frightening howls of the wolves, nor the wind's wail through the majestic fir trees. However, at 15 years old, my lack of experience had decreased my chance of survival on that harsh and bitter night.

I had set out that day to check and reset my animal traps. I waited an extra day for the snowstorm to subside for two reasons: I did not want to meet any ravenous wild animals foraging for food, and I thought my trapping business would be more profitable if I allowed the game more time to hunt. I prepared a sack lunch and put on my hunting belt complete with a hatchet and bullets for my gun. My dog Kenai, part malamute and part wolf, waited impatiently at the door while I packed. This was Kenai's first all-day outing.

Kenai enjoyed the smell of beaver, mouse, and chipmunk. We collected potential pelts that would be sold to the fur traders, ate lunch, and tramped in the woods for hours. At dusk, I knew we should venture home. I whistled for Kenai. Bang! Bang! Suddenly Kenai's cry erupted through the frigid air and fear pierced my heart.

Minutes seemed like hours as I ran to Kenai. My best friend lay in a pool of his own blood, breathing a low, throaty growl. Now I was the one who was frightened! He depended on me to save his life.

Trying to stay calm and rational, I made a plan. With my knowledge of first aid, I fashioned a make-shift tourniquet out of my hunting belt to stop the bleeding. Next, I would attempt to take Kenai home. But how?

 GO ON

● **Lesson 14: Fiction (cont.)**

I decided to make a sled from tree limbs and the inner lining of my parka. I frantically slashed away at the limbs, slipped them inside the lining, zipped it up, and stuffed it with boughs. Cautiously I laid Kenai in the middle, hoping my idea would be successful. Dragging the heavy dog in the frigid night took a toll on my body. The familiar sounds of the forest kept me moving until I dropped from sheer exhaustion. I decided to rest for just a minute. I woke up from a deep sleep startled to hear human voices. Dad and a rescue team had followed my trap lines and found us barely breathing, but conscious!

Neither Kenai nor I will ever forget that night. But because of it, the wolf-like dog and I share a bond of friendship that few people, or dogs, ever experience.

1. **What could be another title for this story?**
   - (A) A Harrowing Hunting Trip
   - (B) Fun in the Woods
   - (C) Dad Saves All!
   - (D) Kenai, the Wonder Dog!

2. **Which of the following was not packed for the trip?**
   - (F) hatchet
   - (G) sack lunch
   - (H) first-aid kit
   - (J) bullets

3. **The narrator of the story probably did not have previous knowledge of what?**
   - (A) first-aid
   - (B) using a gun
   - (C) setting traps
   - (D) saving a dog's life

4. **Which of the following is an opinion based on the information in the story?**
   - (F) The narrator spends time outdoors.
   - (G) The narrator knows how to use a gun.
   - (H) The narrator probably gets good grades in school.
   - (J) The narrator cares for his dog.

5. **The author of this story builds suspense by—**
   - (A) saying the character has a gun.
   - (B) saying that the character's dad rescued him.
   - (C) describing the struggles of the character and his dog.
   - (D) letting the reader know the dog was frightened.

6. **Which of the following events would be last if placed in order?**
   - (F) Remove the lining from the coat.
   - (G) Drag the injured animal to safety.
   - (H) Stuff the lining with boughs and limbs from a tree.
   - (J) Place the injured animal on the lining.

READING: READING COMPREHENSION

● Lesson 15: Fiction

Directions: Read each item. Choose the best answer for each question.

Example

Silently, I surveyed the 100-foot tall vessel from a safe distance. Lying ever so snug to the warm, summer ground, I was concealed from its sight in the tall, yellowing, prairie grass. Numerous landing columns supported its massive, spherical, main control cabin. Red and white lights, rhythmically pulsated around the cabin.

A. **How tall is the vessel?**
- Ⓐ 10 feet
- Ⓑ 100 inches
- Ⓒ 1000 feet
- Ⓓ 100 feet

Skim the passage then read the questions. Refer back to the passage to find the answers. You don't have to reread the story for each question.

● Practice

The Rookie

It was like a dream come true. All through high school Bill had worked on his brother's stock cars hoping that someday he would be allowed to drive in a real race. For years he helped the maintenance crew water and pack the track. Finally, his patience paid off! As an eighteen-year-old senior, he would be the youngest driver ever to race on a popular, new dirt track.

Finally, the green flag came down, and the race was officially underway. During the first couple of laps, Bill carefully felt his way around the track, intent on maintaining his position. Feeling increasingly confident, he passed another car, this time on the inside of the track. "Wow!" he thought. "I really can do this!" But even before this thought had time to clear his mind, the car ahead of him lost a right, rear wheel. Taking a deep breath, Bill muttered to himself, "Phew! What will happen next?"

The red flag came out, and the tow truck removed the disabled car from the track. The racing officials lined up the cars for a restart. Bill found he had moved up three places. Confidently, Bill stepped on it at just the right moment. Dirt flew and engines roared as the drivers challenged each other for position. With only five laps left in the race, Bill was now in fourth place. He did not see the huge hole going into turn two, and he hit it at full speed! The car bounced up on two wheels and headed straight for a light pole at the track's edge. The force of the crash caused the windshield to pop out, just as Bill's head snapped forward. So much for "I can do it!" Bill thought, as he regained his senses.

GO ON

READING: READING COMPREHENSION

● Lesson 15: Fiction (cont.)

Bill graduated from high school with a broken nose, two black eyes, and a swollen lip, twice its normal size. Bill had learned some valuable lessons from his first night of racing. First, he learned to make sure his seat belt was tightly fastened. Bill was also able to verify what he already knew; racing was in his blood.

1. **What is the main idea of this story?**
   - (A) Bill has a lot to learn about racing.
   - (B) Bill loves to race.
   - (C) Bill was very lucky.
   - (D) Bill is not very good at racing.

2. **After the first accident what color flag came out?**
   - (F) checkered
   - (G) green
   - (H) yellow
   - (J) red

3. **What do you think Bill is going to do after graduation?**
   - (A) He will go to work with his father.
   - (B) He will practice stock car racing.
   - (C) He will go to college.
   - (D) He will never race again.

4. **Which of the following would not be Bill's opinion about racing?**
   - (F) Racing is dangerous.
   - (G) Racing is exciting.
   - (H) Racing is easy.
   - (J) Racing requires practice.

5. **What do we know about the main character of this story from the first paragraph?**
   - (A) Bill is excited about racing.
   - (B) Bill does not like stock cars.
   - (C) Bill does not like to work.
   - (D) Bill enjoys going to school.

6. **Bill did not graduate with which one of the following?**
   - (F) black eyes
   - (G) honors
   - (H) swollen lip
   - (J) broken nose

STOP

Name _____ Date_____

● **Directions:** Read each item. Choose the sentence that best answers each question.

Example

Many countries have professional cricket teams. Popular cricket players are national heroes, and a few have even been knighted by the Queen of England! Cricket lovers from Jamaica to New Zealand and from India to England have made the game one of the world's most popular sports.

A.   **What sport has players that have been knighted by the Queen of England?**

(A) soccer
(B) tennis
(C) softball
(D) cricket

Skim the passage then read the questions. Refer back to the passage to find the answers. You don't have to reread the story for each question.

The Story of Color

Imagine a world where everything is either black, white, or gray. Without the blue of the sky or the red of an apple, life would be dull. But if you look outside just after a sunset, the colors of the buildings, trees, and sky fade. Everything does look gray. At night the world seems to have no color at all. But you know the grass is still green at night, even though you can't see the color. Why are things colored at all and why do colors seem to change when the light changes?

Light is made up of waves, a little like waves on an ocean. Each color is a different kind of wave, and the light we see is made up of seven colors—red, orange, yellow, green, blue, indigo and violet. Light usually looks white because all the different waves travel in different directions and mix together. But a special piece of glass, called a prism, can separate the white light into its seven colors. Raindrops sometimes act like prisms too. So when the sun shines during a rain shower, the raindrops separate the sunlight into its colors, making a rainbow.

When white light shines on an object, the object soaks up, or absorbs, some of the light. The rest of the light is bounced back, or reflected. But not all objects reflect the light in the same ways. A red apple, for example, absorbs all the light waves except the red ones. It reflects the red light waves back to our eyes, so we see the color of the apple as red. An orange only reflects orange light and absorbs the rest. Grass reflects only green light waves. So the color of an object is the color of the light waves it reflects. White objects don't absorb any light at all. They reflect all of the light that strikes them.

When only a little light shines on an object, it cannot reflect enough light for our eyes to see its color. That is why everything looks gray or black at night. We need the sun's light to help us see all the wonderful colors around us.

GO ON

READING COMPREHENSON
SAMPLE TEST (cont.)

1. **Light is made up of what?**
   - (A) prisms
   - (B) colors
   - (C) waves
   - (D) sound

2. **What is used to separate light?**
   - (F) filter
   - (G) prism
   - (H) glass
   - (J) shades

3. **If there were no colors, how would life be?**
   - (A) dull
   - (B) blind
   - (C) dark
   - (D) fun

4. **What is needed to help us see color?**
   - (F) eyeglasses
   - (G) sunlight
   - (H) objects
   - (J) charts

5. **What is the function of a prism?**
   - (A) absorbs colors
   - (B) reflects colors
   - (C) separates colors
   - (D) change colors

6. **The light we see is made up of how many colors?**
   - (F) one
   - (G) three
   - (H) five
   - (J) seven

STOP

READING COMPREHENSON
SAMPLE TEST (cont.)

● **Directions:** Read each item. Choose the sentence that best answers each question.

Example

I decided to wait out the blizzard. I had to protect myself by building an igloo around my snowmobile. Busily I packed snow and placed makeshift snow blocks all around. Frightened and exhausted, I lay down and waited for the blizzard to subside.

A. **The narrator of the story protected himself by—**
- (A) climbing a tree.
- (B) laying down and waiting for the blizzard to subside.
- (C) building a fire.
- (D) building an igloo.

Skim the passage then read the questions. Refer back to the passage to find the answers. You don't have to reread the story for each question.

A Country Night

Gazing out my bedroom window at stars I never knew existed, I saw rainbow-colored lights flash across the ink-black sky. The lights seemed to twist and twirl like a kaleidoscope. Surprisingly, they spiraled down just beyond the barn in a clump of trees. Being as curious as the cat that prowled outside my bedroom window, I decided to investigate.

I threw on my clothes, crawled out the window, and tramped through what I hoped was mud in the barnyard. Cautiously I peered out from behind a tree. Three translucent and completely hairless creatures were glaring back at me! I was frozen and speechless. The creatures spoke in what seemed like a variety of strange languages, while manipulating control panels on their belts. Suddenly, their words sounded familiar. My face must have lit up, because they made a final adjustment on their belts and spoke in clear English to me. "What is your name?" I told them my name was Aaron.

They were pretty friendly. The aliens' ship had broken down. Their flight into the galaxy had been turbulent, and some instrument cables had become loosened and frayed. We were all questioning my ability to find some extra parts and repair the damage. I finally accepted the challenge. After all, what else could I do?

Although my uncle's workshop in the back of the barn had enough materials to stock a machine repair shop, it lacked neatness. The aliens' flashlight-like eyes soon spied some promising cables that we took back to their spaceship. After hours of trial, and many trips back and forth to the barn, their spacecraft was ready for lift-off. They asked me to travel through space with them. I considered this unlikely escape from Clarksville and reluctantly declined their invitation. I was beginning to like it here. Before flying off, they gave me a prism as a gift of appreciation.

GO ON

READING COMPREHENSON
SAMPLE TEST (cont.)

1. **How did the creatures communicate with Aaron?**

    (A) flashing lights

    (B) facial expressions

    (C) strange languages

    (D) English

2. **What did the creatures look like?**

    (F) tall and slimy

    (G) large and harry

    (H) translucent and hairless

    (J) newborns

3. **How did you know the creatures were friendly?**

    (A) They did not carry weapons.

    (B) They spoke English.

    (C) They left a gift of appreciation.

    (D) They needed Aaron's help.

4. **What was needed to repair the spaceship?**

    (F) cables

    (G) nuts and bolts

    (H) electricity

    (J) welding torch

5. **How was the spaceship damaged?**

    (A) lightning

    (B) turbulence

    (C) meteor

    (D) crashed

6. **Why did Aaron decide to investigate?**

    (F) fear

    (G) anger

    (H) curiosity

    (J) courage

STOP

ANSWER SHEET

STUDENT'S NAME

LAST | FIRST | MI

SCHOOL

TEACHER

FEMALE ◯   MALE ◯

BIRTH DATE

MONTH	DAY	YEAR

JAN ◯
FEB ◯
MAR ◯
APR ◯
MAY ◯
JUN ◯
JUL ◯
AUG ◯
SEP ◯
OCT ◯
NOV ◯
DEC ◯

DAY: (0)(0) ... (1)(1) (2)(2) (3)(3) (4) (5) (6) (7) (8) (9)

YEAR: (0)(1)(2)(3)(4)(5)(6)(7)(8)(9) (5)(6)(7)(8)(9)

Name grid letters A–Z in columns.

GRADE
⑥ ⑦ ⑧

Part 1: VOCABULARY

A Ⓐ Ⓑ Ⓒ Ⓓ
B Ⓕ Ⓖ Ⓗ Ⓙ

1 Ⓐ Ⓑ Ⓒ Ⓓ
2 Ⓕ Ⓖ Ⓗ Ⓙ
3 Ⓐ Ⓑ Ⓒ Ⓓ
4 Ⓕ Ⓖ Ⓗ Ⓙ
5 Ⓐ Ⓑ Ⓒ Ⓓ
6 Ⓕ Ⓖ Ⓗ Ⓙ
7 Ⓐ Ⓑ Ⓒ Ⓓ
8 Ⓕ Ⓖ Ⓗ Ⓙ
9 Ⓐ Ⓑ Ⓒ Ⓓ
10 Ⓕ Ⓖ Ⓗ Ⓙ
11 Ⓐ Ⓑ Ⓒ Ⓓ
12 Ⓕ Ⓖ Ⓗ Ⓙ
13 Ⓐ Ⓑ Ⓒ Ⓓ
14 Ⓕ Ⓖ Ⓗ Ⓙ
15 Ⓐ Ⓑ Ⓒ Ⓓ
16 Ⓕ Ⓖ Ⓗ Ⓙ
17 Ⓐ Ⓑ Ⓒ Ⓓ
18 Ⓕ Ⓖ Ⓗ Ⓙ
19 Ⓐ Ⓑ Ⓒ Ⓓ
20 Ⓕ Ⓖ Ⓗ Ⓙ
21 Ⓐ Ⓑ Ⓒ Ⓓ
22 Ⓕ Ⓖ Ⓗ Ⓙ
23 Ⓐ Ⓑ Ⓒ Ⓓ
24 Ⓕ Ⓖ Ⓗ Ⓙ
25 Ⓐ Ⓑ Ⓒ Ⓓ
26 Ⓕ Ⓖ Ⓗ Ⓙ
27 Ⓐ Ⓑ Ⓒ Ⓓ
28 Ⓕ Ⓖ Ⓗ Ⓙ
29 Ⓐ Ⓑ Ⓒ Ⓓ
30 Ⓕ Ⓖ Ⓗ Ⓙ
31 Ⓐ Ⓑ Ⓒ Ⓓ
32 Ⓕ Ⓖ Ⓗ Ⓙ
33 Ⓐ Ⓑ Ⓒ Ⓓ
34 Ⓕ Ⓖ Ⓗ Ⓙ
35 Ⓐ Ⓑ Ⓒ Ⓓ
36 Ⓕ Ⓖ Ⓗ Ⓙ
37 Ⓐ Ⓑ Ⓒ Ⓓ
38 Ⓕ Ⓖ Ⓗ Ⓙ

Part 2: READING COMPREHENSION

A Ⓐ Ⓑ Ⓒ Ⓓ
1 Ⓐ Ⓑ Ⓒ Ⓓ
2 Ⓕ Ⓖ Ⓗ Ⓙ
3 Ⓐ Ⓑ Ⓒ Ⓓ
4 Ⓕ Ⓖ Ⓗ Ⓙ
5 Ⓐ Ⓑ Ⓒ Ⓓ
6 Ⓕ Ⓖ Ⓗ Ⓙ
7 Ⓐ Ⓑ Ⓒ Ⓓ
8 Ⓕ Ⓖ Ⓗ Ⓙ
9 Ⓐ Ⓑ Ⓒ Ⓓ
10 Ⓕ Ⓖ Ⓗ Ⓙ
11 Ⓐ Ⓑ Ⓒ Ⓓ
12 Ⓕ Ⓖ Ⓗ Ⓙ

1-57768-977-1 — Spectrum Test Practice 7

Name _____ Date _____

READING PRACTICE TEST

● **Part 1: Vocabulary**

Directions: Read each item. Choose the answer that means the same or about the same as the underlined word.

Examples

A. He was not one to <u>boast</u>.

    Ⓐ brag
    Ⓑ complain
    Ⓒ promise
    Ⓓ comment

B. He was very <u>solemn</u> for his age.

    Ⓕ smart
    Ⓖ serious
    Ⓗ silly
    Ⓙ slow

If you are not sure which answer is correct, take your best guess. Eliminate answer choices you know are wrong.

1. The statement left him <u>puzzled</u>.

    Ⓐ angry
    Ⓑ confused
    Ⓒ laughing
    Ⓓ broken

2. The meaning was <u>significant</u>.

    Ⓕ shallow
    Ⓖ serious
    Ⓗ important
    Ⓙ thoughtful

3. He had no <u>qualms</u> about the trip.

    Ⓐ questions
    Ⓑ worries
    Ⓒ answers
    Ⓓ excitement

4. She had an <u>adverse</u> reaction to the medication.

    Ⓕ unfavorable
    Ⓖ uncomfortable
    Ⓗ odd
    Ⓙ average

5. Did you <u>extinguish</u> the candle?

    Ⓐ light
    Ⓑ change
    Ⓒ put out
    Ⓓ purchase

6. The lion was <u>fierce</u>.

    Ⓕ ferocious
    Ⓖ friendly
    Ⓗ hungry
    Ⓙ asleep

7. He did not <u>imply</u> otherwise.

    Ⓐ answer
    Ⓑ suggest
    Ⓒ question
    Ⓓ search

8. She did so with <u>delight</u>.

    Ⓕ dread
    Ⓖ fear
    Ⓗ joy
    Ⓙ displeasure

GO ON

Read each item. Choose the answer that means the opposite of the underlined word.

9. He was always <u>punctual</u>.
   - (A) tardy
   - (B) perfect
   - (C) rough
   - (D) natural

10. She hoped to <u>borrow</u> the money.
    - (F) steal
    - (G) uncover
    - (H) lend
    - (J) find

11. He was happy to be a contest <u>finalist</u>.
    - (A) winner
    - (B) loser
    - (C) participant
    - (D) player

12. The trophy was <u>tarnished</u>.
    - (F) unpolished
    - (G) polished
    - (H) destroyed
    - (J) antique

13. Her <u>anticipation</u> was shared by others.
    - (A) dread
    - (B) participation
    - (C) contribution
    - (D) disposition

14. The assignment was <u>tedious</u>.
    - (F) boring
    - (G) dull
    - (H) exciting
    - (J) difficult

15. She would not <u>accept</u> the challenge.
    - (A) examine
    - (B) explore
    - (C) decline
    - (D) allow

16. She was always <u>courteous</u>.
    - (F) brave
    - (G) correct
    - (H) right
    - (J) rude

17. His motives were <u>questionable</u>.
    - (A) extreme
    - (B) certain
    - (C) quiet
    - (D) correct

18. It was a <u>swift</u> trip.
    - (F) short
    - (G) safe
    - (H) slow
    - (J) boring

GO ON

Name _____ Date _____

Read each item. Choose the correct meaning for each underlined word.

19. The meeting was brief.
- (A) informative
- (B) short
- (C) scheduled
- (D) needless

20. She had to hide her score.
- (F) animal skin
- (G) conceal
- (H) beat
- (J) find

21. He was hesitant to address the crowd.
- (A) direct
- (B) speak to
- (C) number
- (D) move

22. She was not as lean as she once was.
- (F) skinny
- (G) mean
- (H) brave
- (J) happy

23. The plot was full of intrigue.
- (A) field
- (B) scheme
- (C) lot
- (D) story

24. He couldn't place him.
- (F) recognize
- (G) put
- (H) find
- (J) beat

25. She was able to monitor their progress.
- (A) screen
- (B) track
- (C) assist a teacher
- (D) mouse

26. They chose to boot him out.
- (F) kick
- (G) shoe
- (H) basic training
- (J) bring

27. How did you know he was right?
- (A) bright
- (B) smart
- (C) correct
- (D) left

28. What a good deed!
- (F) legal document
- (G) action
- (H) meal
- (J) signature

GO ON

READING PRACTICE TEST
Part 1: Vocabulary (cont.)

Read each item. Find the word that fits each blank the best.

29. I'm afraid to try. Can you _____ me?

- (A) coax
- (B) make
- (C) let
- (D) find

30. The friends are not the same, but the two do have some _____.

- (F) differences
- (G) similarities
- (H) problems
- (J) questions

31. A caterpillar makes an amazing _____ to a butterfly.

- (A) cocoon
- (B) transformation
- (C) presentation
- (D) relation

32. Making honey is the _____ of the very experienced bee.

- (F) experience
- (G) joy
- (H) passion
- (J) expertise

33. I know all the _____ for science, but I can't spell those words.

- (A) answers
- (B) questions
- (C) terminology
- (D) mutations

34. The inventor has a new _____ to play.

- (F) game
- (G) novelty
- (H) newt
- (J) notion

35. He was used to the fruitful and _____ farmlands of Iowa.

- (A) fertile
- (B) fruitless
- (C) slanted
- (D) huge

36. The house next door is _____, but a family will be moving in soon.

- (F) beautiful
- (G) big
- (H) vacant
- (J) sold

37. When my friend moved away, she gave me a nice _____ to read.

- (A) letter
- (B) smile
- (C) goodbye
- (D) keepsake

38. I will need to set up my _____ to complete my painting assignment.

- (F) computer
- (G) theme
- (H) easel
- (J) schedule

STOP

Name _____ Date_____

● **Part 2: Reading Comprehension**

Directions: Read each item. Choose the best answer for each question.

Example

Lead glass is made by using lead oxide in place of lime to produce glass of fine quality. Lead glass is used to make lenses for eyeglasses, telescopes, and microscopes. Radio and television tubes as well as the tubing in neon signs are also made with this glass.	**A. What is used in place of lime to produce glass of fine quality?** Ⓐ diamonds Ⓑ sand Ⓒ lead oxide Ⓓ neon

Skim the passage then read the questions. Refer back to the passage to find the answers. You don't have to reread the story for each question.

Accidents, Dreams, and Discoveries

Many people think that scientists make great discoveries only while they are working hard in a laboratory. But sometimes scientists, mathematicians, and inventors find the answers to difficult problems while they are relaxing or even sleeping.

For example, the great physicist Isaac Newton had been trying for a long time to discover the laws of gravity. For a while his work went well. But then he seemed to come to a dead end. Finally, he decided to forget his work and relax for just one day. As he sat under an apple tree, enjoying the warm, pleasant afternoon, an apple fell from the tree and landed on the ground in front of him. Of course, Newton had seen apples fall from trees before. This time, though, the falling apple gave him the clue he needed, and the last of the laws of gravity fell into place, too.

As you can see, the most ordinary things can help scientists make discoveries. The French mathematician, Rene Descartes, sat one day

watching a fly walk on his ceiling. Instead of swatting the fly, he watched it cross the ceiling, come to a corner, and walk down the wall. In his imagination, Descartes drew a line following the fly's path. As the line crossed the corner of the wall, Descartes thought of the perfect way to make pictures of mathematical equations on graph paper. The method that he and the fly invented is still used today.

Sometimes even dreams can lead to inventions. Elias Howe had been trying for a long time to invent a sewing machine. But he could not quite make his machine work. After another long day of failure, Howe gave up and went to sleep. That night he dreamed that he was being chased by men carrying spears. But these strange spears had holes in the points. When Elias woke up, he remembered the dream, and his problem was solved. He put the eye of the sewing machine needle at the pointed end, and his invention worked!

GO ON ▷

1. **What is surprising about some great scientific discoveries?**

    (A) how much time is spent working in laboratories

    (B) scientists not sharing information

    (C) that they can happen while relaxing or even sleeping

    (D) how much reading is required

2. **How did Elias Howe solve the problem with his invention, the sewing machine?**

    (F) he watched his mother sew

    (G) he spoke with other inventors

    (H) he had a dream

    (J) he drew pictures

3. **What is a useful tool for solving difficult problems?**

    (A) never give up

    (B) read everything ever written on the subject

    (C) relaxing, or even sleeping

    (D) talking to a friend

4. **Isaac Newton studied in what field?**

    (F) botany

    (G) physics

    (H) apple orchard

    (J) corn field

5. **Rene Descartes thought of what way to make pictures of mathematical equations?**

    (A) watching flies

    (B) connecting dots

    (C) using graph paper

    (D) eating an apple

6. **What had Isaac Newton been trying to do for a long time?**

    (F) take a break

    (G) pick apples

    (H) drop an apple from a tree

    (J) discover the laws of gravity

GO ON

═══ READING PRACTICE TEST ═══

● **Part 2: Reading Comprehension (cont.)**

Directions: Read the paragraph below. Choose the sentence that best answers the question.

Example

Megan felt uneasy as they turned off the highway onto the gravel. She wanted to slow down, but Tim and Justin were quite far ahead. Not wanting to be left behind in a cloud of dust, she raced forward on the winding gravel road.	**A. Why didn't Megan slow down?** (A) She liked gravel roads. (B) She liked winding roads. (C) She wanted to create a cloud of dust. (D) She didn't want to be left in a cloud of dust.

Skim the passage then read the questions. Refer back to the passage to find the answers. You don't have to reread the story for each question.

Corrals in the Heavens

The spirited orange, yellow, and red flames reached upward toward the starry sky from the crackling campfire. It was nearly midnight. Cathy and Stacey were sprawled out around the campfire, carefully roasting the remaining marshmallows to a perfect bubbly brown. The girls resisted the need to end a perfect day.

Cathy and Stacy had been best friends since first grade. During their summer vacations, they were particularly attracted to horse-related activities. Cathy and Stacey had received their horses on the same Christmas four years earlier.

Now that Cathy and Stacey were in junior high, their parents knew they were responsible enough for trail-riding and camping together. Stacey's dad had made arrangements to borrow a double horse trailer to transport the horses to Loud Thunder Forest Preserve. The horses quickly greeted each other as friends in this long-awaited rendezvous.

"Look at that Big Dipper!" Cathy's father noticed as he pointed up to the late evening sky. "It looks like it's pouring a drink for your horses."

"There we are Stacey," whispered Cathy, pointing to the stars. "We're riding our horses on that star next to the Big Dipper. We better be cautious of that Great Bear and her Little Bear cub."

"Let's leap to that neighboring bright star to avoid spooking the horses," added Stacey, quickly joining the inventive fantasy game.

The girls continued their journey, each trying to out-best the other with her fantasy. Together they rode their horses from one constellation to another, escaping lions and bears.

Finally, the girls exhausted the game and the campsite became quiet. They couldn't resist their heavy, drooping eyelids and finally agreed to enter the tent for the night. They knew that early morning would bring a real-life riding adventure.

GO ON ⟩

READING PRACTICE TEST
Part 2: Reading Comprehension (cont.)

Read each item. Choose the sentence that best answers each question.

7. **How did Cathy and Stacey resist the need to end a perfect day?**
   - Ⓐ They went horseback riding.
   - Ⓑ They went camping.
   - Ⓒ They pretended to ride horses on the stars.
   - Ⓓ They read by firelight.

8. **Cathy and Stacey had been best friends—**
   - Ⓕ since the Christmas they both received horses.
   - Ⓖ since the first grade.
   - Ⓗ since last summer.
   - Ⓙ since they were born.

9. **What made the girls continue their game?**
   - Ⓐ They weren't ready for sleep.
   - Ⓑ They were trying to out-best one another.
   - Ⓒ Their horses were restless.
   - Ⓓ There were so many stars in the late evening sky.

10. **A constellation is—**
   - Ⓕ a horse trailer.
   - Ⓖ a tent.
   - Ⓗ a group of stars.
   - Ⓙ drooping eyelids.

11. **What kind of journey did the girls take that evening?**
   - Ⓐ They took a real life riding adventure.
   - Ⓑ They played an inventive fantasy game.
   - Ⓒ They rode in a double horse trailer.
   - Ⓓ They made a long awaited rendezvous.

12. **Why did the campsite become quiet?**
   - Ⓕ The horses were asleep.
   - Ⓖ The fire had died down.
   - Ⓗ The girls had exhausted the game.
   - Ⓙ Their parents asked them to be quiet.

STOP

LANGUAGE: LANGUAGE MECHANICS

● Lesson 1: Punctuation

Directions: Mark the space for the punctuation mark that is needed in the sentence. Mark the space for "none" if no more punctuation marks are needed.

Examples

A. **What time is it**
- (A) .
- (B) !
- (C) ?
- (D) none

B. **When I graduate from high school I plan to go to college.**
- (F) ?
- (G) ,
- (H) !
- (J) none

 Clue Read the sentence, look at the answer choices, then read the sentence again. See if any of the punctuation marks are needed in the sentence.

● Practice

1. **Fortunately I've been studying hard all year.**
- (A) "
- (B) !
- (C) ,
- (D) none

2. **"Are you planning on going to college? asked James**
- (F) ?
- (G) "
- (H) ,
- (J) none

3. **His favorite subjects are math history and science.**
- (A) "
- (B) ,
- (C) !
- (D) none

4. **"What kind of question is that" the teacher asked.**
- (F) !
- (G) ?
- (H) ,
- (J) none

5. **The class read The Tell-Tale Heart."**
- (A) "
- (B) ,
- (C) :
- (D) none

6. **"Did you enjoy the story?" asked her teacher.**
- (F) ?
- (G) "
- (H) ,
- (J) none

GO ON

LANGUAGE: LANGUAGE MECHANICS

● **Lesson 1: Punctuation (cont.)**

For 7–12, read each answer. Fill in the space for the choice that has a punctuation error. If there is no mistake, fill in the fourth answer space.

7. (A) It was long after midnight
    (B) before they found their way
    (C) to the campsite where the others slept.
    (D) no mistakes

8. (F) Michael, the team captain
    (G) gave each of the players
    (H) a chance to participate.
    (J) no mistakes

9. (A) "How could you be so cruel,"
    (B) asked Phoebe, trying hard
    (C) not to cry.
    (D) no mistakes

10. (F) 254 Glendora Ave.
    (G) Long Beach CA 90803
    (H) May 30, 2003
    (J) no mistakes

11. (A) Dear Ms. Robertson,
    (B) In response to your inquiry
    (C) we are enclosing our most recent brochure.
    (D) no mistakes

12. (F) We trust it will answer all of your questions.
    (G) Sincerely,
    (H) John Smith
    (J) no mistakes

For numbers 13 and 14, read each sentence. Choose the word or words that fit best in the blank and show the correct punctuation.

13. **"Is that word in the _____ inquired James.**
    (A) dictionary
    (B) dictionary,
    (C) dictionary?
    (D) dictionary?"

14. **When the fish jumped out of the _____ we realized it was huge.**
    (F) water
    (G) water;
    (H) water,
    (J) water.

STOP

LANGUAGE: LANGUAGE MECHANICS

● Lesson 2: Capitalization and Punctuation

Directions: Mark the space for the answer that shows correct punctuation and capitalization. Mark the space for "correct as it is" if the underlined part is correct.

Examples

A.
- Ⓐ "Can we go to the park, asked Karen?
- Ⓑ "If you have finished your homework," answered her mother.
- Ⓒ "I finished all my homework! exclaimed Karen.
- Ⓓ Mother said be home in time for dinner.

B. Sally knew both <u>Karen and Tom.</u>
- Ⓕ Karen, and Tom
- Ⓖ Karen and, Tom
- Ⓗ Karen: and Tom
- Ⓙ correct as it is

 Clue Remember, you are looking for the answer that shows correct capitalization and punctuation. If you are not sure which answer is correct, take your best guess.

● Practice

1.
- Ⓐ The teacher asked, "Did you complete the assignment?"
- Ⓑ "I did not," replied jared. "I left my book in class."
- Ⓒ "Can I turn it in tomorrow" asked Jared.
- Ⓓ "Yes, however it will be marked late, said the teacher.

2.
- Ⓕ He flew from Boston Massachusetts, to New york New york.
- Ⓖ On Tuesday, he will fly back to Boston.
- Ⓗ there he will meet with Mr. Charles Gainey.
- Ⓙ Until now, he had only spoken with Mr. gainey on the telephone.

3.
- Ⓐ Early on Saturday, the first of October, Michael began his new job.
- Ⓑ Tuesday and thursday morning he attends classes.
- Ⓒ His best friend, senator Richard harwood, encouraged his participation.
- Ⓓ His sister, susan was also very encouraging.

4. Have you ever sailed on <u>lake michigan</u>
- Ⓕ Lake michigan?
- Ⓖ lake Michigan.
- Ⓗ Lake Michigan?
- Ⓙ correct as it is

5. She has her <u>mothers</u> eyes.
- Ⓐ mother's
- Ⓑ mothers'
- Ⓒ Mothers
- Ⓓ correct as it is

 GO ON

Name _____ Date _____

LANGUAGE: LANGUAGE MECHANICS

● **Lesson 2: Capitalization and Punctuation (cont.)**

6. **We just finished studying the <u>french revolution</u>.**
   - (F) French revolution
   - (G) French Revolution
   - (H) french Revolution
   - (J) correct as it is

7.
   - (A) Last Saturday which was May 25
   - (B) my brother William married Suzanne.
   - (C) The happy couple, William and Suzanne, were married at last!
   - (D) When rev. benson finally introduced Mr and Mrs. Jones, I wanted to cheer.

8.
   - (F) In northwest cambodia, not far from its border with thailand,
   - (G) lies the ruined city of angkor.
   - (H) From about 880 to 1225, Angkor was the capital of the mighty Khmer Empire.
   - (J) Angkor was abandoned about 1434 and the capital was moved to phnon penh.

9. **Galileo, an <u>italian astronomer and physicist</u>, was born on February 15, 1564.**
   - (A) Italian Astronomer and Physicist
   - (B) italian Astronomer and Physicist
   - (C) Italian astronomer and physicist
   - (D) correct as it is

10. **Will <u>dad pick up mother</u> at the train station?**
    - (F) Dad pick up Mother
    - (G) dad pick up Mother
    - (H) Dad pick up mother
    - (J) correct as it is

11. **After we ate _____ did our homework.**
    - (A) dinner, we
    - (B) Dinner, we
    - (C) dinner We
    - (D) dinner, We

12. **Rolls, bagels, _____ are displayed in the bakery.**
    - (F) scones, and muffins,
    - (G) scones, and muffins
    - (H) scones and muffins;
    - (J) scones and muffins,

13. **Its location, _____ was breathtaking.**
    - (A) on the shore,
    - (B) on the shore
    - (C) on the shore:
    - (D) On the shore

14. **Cutting with a dull knife is _____**
    - (F) dangerous!
    - (G) Dangerous!
    - (H) dangerous?
    - (J) Dangerous?

STOP

LANGUAGE MECHANICS
SAMPLE TEST

● **Directions:** Mark the space for the punctuation mark that is needed in the sentence. Mark the space for "none" if no more punctuation marks are needed.

Examples

A. What are your plans for summer vacation.

   (A) .
   (B) !
   (C) ?
   (D) :

B. Until now he had not given much thought to summer activities.

   (F) ?
   (G) "
   (H) !
   (J) ,

---

1. "You look pretty, said her mother.

   (A) !
   (B) ;
   (C) "
   (D) ?

2. Rivers lakes and streams make great camping sites.

   (F) !
   (G) ?
   (H) "
   (J) ,

3. Ouch That hurt.

   (A) !
   (B) ,
   (C) ;
   (D) .

4. When do we have to go

   (F) .
   (G) ?
   (H) !
   (J) "

5. The light was too dim for reading

   (A) !
   (B) ?
   (C) .
   (D) ,

6. Giving blood doesnt hurt and can save lives.

   (F) !
   (G) '
   (H) ;
   (J) ,

GO ON

Name _____   Date _____

Mark the space for the answer that shows correct punctuation and capitalization.

7. **Do you tend to take out your anger by blaming _____**
   - Ⓐ People?
   - Ⓑ people?
   - Ⓒ people!
   - Ⓓ People.

8. **"Is that the new dress you plan to _____ inquired Kate.**
   - Ⓕ wear,
   - Ⓖ wear
   - Ⓗ wear?
   - Ⓙ wear?"

9. **They were best friends through thick and thin.**
   - Ⓐ thick, and thin.
   - Ⓑ thick and, thin.
   - Ⓒ thick: and thin.
   - Ⓓ correct as it is

10. **Her shoes were the wrong color the wrong size, and they pinched her toes.**
    - Ⓕ color, the
    - Ⓖ color: the
    - Ⓗ color; the
    - Ⓙ correct as it is

11. **He worked in a building with a garden on the roof.**
    - Ⓐ building; with
    - Ⓑ building, with
    - Ⓒ building: with
    - Ⓓ correct as it is

12. **"It was not always this difficult, sighed Helen.**
    - Ⓕ Difficult," sighed
    - Ⓖ difficult, Sighed
    - Ⓗ difficult," sighed
    - Ⓙ difficult" sighed

13. **She answered without hesitation or regret.**
    - Ⓐ Hesitation or Regret.
    - Ⓑ hesitation, or regret.
    - Ⓒ hesitation or, regret.
    - Ⓓ correct as it is

14. **The assignment should include _____ table of contents, page numbers, and glossary.**
    - Ⓕ the following:
    - Ⓖ the following,
    - Ⓗ the following;
    - Ⓙ the following

GO ON

Name _____   Date _____

Mark the space for the choice that has a punctuation or capitalization error. If all of the answers are correct, mark "correct as it is."

15.
- (A) When you have an idea that is perfectly clear to you
- (B) it ought to be easy to make it perfectly clear to someone else.
- (C) Right?
- (D) correct as it is

16.
- (F) Do you try to present your ideas in words that your listeners can easily relate to?
- (G) Do you consider your listeners' opinions and
- (H) prejudices when attempting to get their attention.
- (J) correct as it is

17.
- (A) Mr. John Anderson
- (B) 1856 Broadway Ave.
- (C) Long Beach CA 90815
- (D) correct as it is

18.
- (F) Dear Mr. Anderson,
- (G) In response to your inquiry,
- (H) the position has been filled.
- (J) correct as it is

19.
- (A) Your qualifications are impressive.
- (B) we will keep your application on file for two years
- (C) in the event an opening becomes available.
- (D) correct as it is

20.
- (F) Thank you for your interest in our company.
- (G) Sincerely
- (H) James Abbot
- (J) correct as it is

21.
- (A) Some people, when they are angry
- (B) tend to lash out at the people closest to them.
- (C) This often leads to hurt feelings.
- (D) correct as it is

22.
- (F) Being tactful and diplomatic are important qualities.
- (G) But tact and diplomacy alone arent enough to get the job done.
- (H) You must also be brave.
- (J) correct as it is

STOP

Name _____ Date _____

LANGUAGE: LANGUAGE EXPRESSION

● **Lesson 3: Usage**

Directions: Read the directions for each section. Select the best answer for each question.

Examples

Choose the word or phrase that best completes the sentence.	Choose the answer that is a complete and correctly written sentence.
A. _____ ever been in a situation that was really frightening?	B.
(A) have you	(F) I don't want to leave any fingerprints.
(B) Have you	(G) The moon pass between the earth and the sun.
(C) has you	(H) There were no rain all summer.
(D) Has you	(J) The shop was given away ice cream.

 Clue If you are unsure which answer is the correct choice, say each one to yourself. The right answer usually sounds best.

● **Practice**

For numbers 1–3, choose the word or phrase that best completes the sentence.

1. **The American soldiers _____ poorly fed and supplied.**
   (A) was
   (B) is
   (C) were
   (D) wasn't

2. **The snow, _____ quickly melted, flooded the driveway.**
   (F) which
   (G) who
   (H) where
   (J) what

3. **The company _____ home soon.**
   (A) will go
   (B) will went
   (C) went
   (D) don't go

For numbers 4–6, choose the answer that is a complete and correctly written sentence.

4.
   (F) Elephants is different from one another.
   (G) They are very friendlier in Japan.
   (H) We should learn about other culture to understand others.
   (J) His goal was to find the tomb of King Tut.

5.
   (A) Archaeologists seen to lead exciting lives.
   (B) The weather this spring is exceptionally warm and dry.
   (C) The firefighter were honored for her courageousness.
   (D) His new puppy was very play.

 GO ON

LANGUAGE: LANGUAGE EXPRESSION

● Lesson 3: Usage (cont.)

6.
- (F) Many birds construct nests in tree branch.
- (G) Potato grow underground.
- (H) Our school chorus needs two sopranos to sing the duet.
- (J) I likes to watch college football games.

For numbers 7–11, Read each answer choice. Fill in the space for the choice that has a usage error. If there is no mistake, fill in the fourth answer space.

7.
- (A) People have been
- (B) interested in birds
- (C) since the beginning of time.
- (D) no mistakes

8.
- (F) The nest of the smallest bird in the world,
- (G) the bee hummingbird,
- (H) is less than two inch high.
- (J) no mistakes

9.
- (A) It were warm this morning,
- (B) but the temperature has been dropping rapidly
- (C) all afternoon.
- (D) no mistakes

10.
- (F) A group of people who gather to hear something,
- (G) such as a speech,
- (H) is an audience.
- (J) no mistakes

11.
- (A) The circus acrobat swung from a trapeze,
- (B) dropped to a trampoline below,
- (C) and landed grace on his toes.
- (D) no mistakes

For numbers 12–15, choose the best way to write the underlined part of each sentence. If the underlined part is correct, fill in the fourth answer space.

12. The band <u>conductor</u> slowly raised her baton.
- (F) conductors
- (G) conduct
- (H) conducted
- (J) correct as it is

13. The swim team <u>were</u> in training four times each week.
- (A) has been
- (B) hadn't
- (C) has
- (D) correct as it is

14. It is important to keep a wound <u>clean</u> in order to prevent infection.
- (F) cleans
- (G) to clean
- (H) cleanest
- (J) correct as it is

15. A full tank of oxygen is a <u>necessary</u> for a deep-sea diver.
- (A) necessity
- (B) necessitate
- (C) needed
- (D) correct as it is

GO ON

● Lesson 3: Usage (cont.)

Read the story below. Use it to answer questions 16–19.

(1) Wild elephants are in danger. (2) In Africa and Asia, the human population has been <u>growing</u>. (3) As a result, more and more people have cleared and settled on land where elephants once lived. (4) The elephants <u>has been</u> crowded into small areas. (5) Because elephants need large areas of land to find enough food to eat, their food supply is shrinking all of the time.

(6) In addition, hunters anxious to make money are killing African elephants for their ivory tusks. (7) The tusks, which sell for over $20,000 a pair, are carved to make <u>beauty</u> works of art. (8) All elephants in the northern and southern sections of Africa have been killed already. (9) There are laws that forbid the killing of elephants in special areas where land has been set aside to safeguard them. (10) But <u>therefore</u> ivory trade can make them wealthy, some hunters shoot elephants anyway.

16. **In sentence 2, <u>growing</u> is best written—**
    - Ⓕ grown
    - Ⓖ growth
    - Ⓗ grows
    - Ⓙ no change

17. **In sentence 4, <u>has been</u> is best written—**
    - Ⓐ is been
    - Ⓑ is being
    - Ⓒ have been
    - Ⓓ no change

18. **In sentence 7, <u>beauty</u> is best written—**
    - Ⓕ beautiful
    - Ⓖ beautifully
    - Ⓗ beauties
    - Ⓙ no change

19. **In sentence 10, <u>therefore</u> is best written—**
    - Ⓐ why
    - Ⓑ where
    - Ⓒ because
    - Ⓓ no change

STOP

LANGUAGE: LANGUAGE EXPRESSION

● Lesson 4: Sentences

Directions: Read the directions for each section. Select the best answer for each question.

Examples

Which word is the simple subject of the sentence?

A.   A (A) <u>large</u> (B) <u>crowd</u> (C) <u>blocked</u> the (D) <u>entryway</u>.

    (A) large

    (B) crowd

    (C) blocked

    (D) entryway

Which answer choice is the best combination of the underlined sentences?

B.   <u>The dog is old. The dog is at the veterinarian.</u>

    (F) The old dog that is at the veterinarian.

    (G) The dog is at the old veterinarian.

    (H) The dog that is at the veterinarian is old.

    (J) The old dog is at the veterinarian.

 Clue If a question is too difficult, skip it and come back to it later.

● Practice

For numbers 1–3, find the underlined part that is the simple subject of the sentence.

1.   The (A) <u>frightened</u> (B) <u>man</u> (C) <u>ran</u> through the (D) <u>trees</u>.

    (A) frightened

    (B) man

    (C) ran

    (D) trees

2.   (F) <u>Three</u> (G) <u>yellow</u> (H) <u>ducklings</u> swam across the (J) <u>pond</u>.

    (F) Three

    (G) yellow

    (H) ducklings

    (J) pond

3.   Happily walking down the (A) <u>sidewalk</u>, the (B) <u>girl</u> (C) <u>ate</u> her (D) <u>ice cream</u> cone.

    (A) sidewalk

    (B) girl

    (C) ate

    (D) ice cream

For numbers 4–6, find the underlined part that is the simple predicate (verb) of the sentence.

4.   The (F) <u>vase</u> (G) <u>fell</u> from the (H) <u>mantel</u> onto the hard (J) <u>floor</u>.

    (F) vase

    (G) fell

    (H) mantel

    (J) floor

GO ON

LANGUAGE: LANGUAGE EXPRESSION

● **Lesson 4: Sentences (cont.)**

5. **Creative and (A) motivated (B) artists (C) paint almost (D) everyday.**

   (A) motivated

   (B) artists

   (C) paint

   (D) everyday

6. **An old, battered (F) car (G) sat on the (H) vacant street (J) next to the curb.**

   (F) car

   (G) sat

   (H) vacant

   (J) next

For numbers 7–10, choose the answer that best combines the underlined sentences.

7. **A friend stopped by our house. The friend had a chocolate cake.**

   (A) A friend stopped by our house with a chocolate cake.

   (B) A friend and chocolate cake stopped by our house.

   (C) A friend carrying a chocolate cake stopped by our house.

   (D) Carrying a chocolate cake a friend stopped by our house.

8. **Andrew went to the store. He went to the store for potato chips.**

   (F) Andrew he went to the store for potato chips.

   (G) The store had potato chips where Andrew went.

   (H) Potato chips were at the store where Andrew went for them.

   (J) Andrew went to the store for potato chips.

9. **Stephanie bought a book. She bought a book about computers. The book was expensive.**

   (A) Stephanie bought a book that was expensive and that was about computers.

   (B) Stephanie bought an expensive book about computers.

   (C) An expensive book about computers was bought by Stephanie.

   (D) She bought an expensive book about computers.

10. **Bill went to the house. Bill is an architect. The architect brought blueprints to the house.**

    (F) The blueprints were brought to the house by the architect.

    (G) Bill is an architect and he brought to the house blueprints.

    (H) Bill, an architect, brought blueprints to the house.

    (J) An architect named Bill brought blueprints.

GO ON

LANGUAGE: LANGUAGE EXPRESSION

● Lesson 4: Sentences (cont.)

Read the story below. Use it to answer questions 11–14.

(1) Behind every good motion picture is a good film editor. (2) A movie is not always filmed in the order it is shown in a theater or on television. (3) All the scenes that is in the same location are shot at the same time. (4) If the beginning and ending of a movie take place in the desert, the scenes are shot one after another. (5) Once the whole movie has been shot, film editors view it and arrange it in the correct order.

(6) Usually, film makers shoot more film than is needed. (7) They cut out parts that don't fit especially well. (8) Sometimes they discover many many parts that seem to drag. (9) They speed up the action by cutting slow scenes. (10) After all of the scenes have been joined in the correct order, the film is ready for presentation. (11) A film editor who has done his or her job well helps to make sure that the movie will be enjoyed by all. (12) A film editor is a very important person.

11. In sentence 3, is is best written—

    (A) are

    (B) aren't

    (C) was

    (D) no change

12. In sentence 5, correct is best written—

    (F) correcting

    (G) corrects

    (H) was corrected

    (J) no change

13. How is sentence 8 best written?

    (A) Parts seem to drag on and they discover this.

    (B) Dragging parts are discovered sometimes.

    (C) Sometimes they discover parts that seem to drag.

    (D) no change

14. Which sentence needlessly repeats an idea?

    (F) 2

    (G) 6

    (H) 11

    (J) 12

STOP

LANGUAGE: LANGUAGE EXPRESSION

● Lesson 5: Paragraphs

Directions: Read the directions for each section. Choose the answer that you think is correct.

Example

Read the paragraph below. Find the best topic sentence for the paragraph.

A. _____. The materials used will determine the structure's appearance. You have probably already seen some buildings made of the most common building materials, which are concrete, steel, brick, and wood.

(A) Buildings can be made from many different materials.

(B) Concrete is the best building material.

(C) Brick is the best looking building material available.

(D) Different climates require different building materials.

 Clue Skim each passage then read the questions. Refer back to the passage to find the answers.

● Practice

Read the paragraph below. Find the best topic sentence for the paragraph.

1. _____. Squirrels make their homes with leaves and twigs high in a tree. Beavers make lodges out of sticks and mud.

(A) Animals do unusual things.

(B) People aren't the only ones who build homes out of materials available to them.

(C) Weather influences what animals do.

(D) Natural materials can be used in many ways.

Find the answer choice that best develops the topic sentence below.

2. The sea otter is a fascinating mammal.

(F) Most sea otters live near the North Pacific Ocean. They have hind feet shaped like flippers. They can stay under water longer than most other mammals!

(G) My sister has a stuffed toy otter. It is very cute!

(H) Some sea otters live on the coast of California. Others can be found in Alaska.

(J) Some people take care of sick sea otters. Others enjoy observing them.

 GO ON

LANGUAGE: LANGUAGE EXPRESSION

● **Lesson 5: Paragraphs (cont.)**

For numbers 3 and 4, read the paragraph. Find the sentence that does not belong in the paragraph.

3. (1) Humankind's mastery of the waves likely had a humble beginning. (2) People have always enjoyed swimming. (3) When our ancient ancestors first encountered a large lake or fast-moving river, they were probably reluctant to get too close. (4) But of course, this fear was overcome.

    Ⓐ Sentence 1
    Ⓑ Sentence 2
    Ⓒ Sentence 3
    Ⓓ Sentence 4

4. **(1) The first castles were built by noblemen who wanted to protect their land. (2) Castles were surrounded by moats filled with water. (3) Castles make us think of knights and fair ladies. (4) Only by lowering the drawbridge could anyone cross the moat.**

    Ⓕ Sentence 1
    Ⓖ Sentence 2
    Ⓗ Sentence 3
    Ⓙ Sentence 4

For numbers 5 and 6, read the paragraph. Find the sentence that best fits the blank in the paragraph.

5. **In the first 74 years of assaults on Everest, 144 lives were lost, an average of less than two lives a year. _____. The increasing commercialization of Everest can be blamed. Guides charge high fees to haul climbers of questionable skills up and down the mountain.**

    Ⓐ Souvenir shops are found along the way.
    Ⓑ Many people have a wonderful experience climbing Everest.
    Ⓒ Ban oxygen at the summit and the problem is solved.
    Ⓓ In a single season in the 1990s, 12 people died in their attempts to climb Everest.

6. **Golden Retrievers are known for their eagerness to please their human owners, and they love to stay close to them. _____. Golden Retrievers do not like being left alone and can develop separation anxiety.**

    Ⓕ Their coats need to be brushed often.
    Ⓖ They like to eat table scraps.
    Ⓗ They are just as friendly to strangers.
    Ⓙ They like to have their own space to sleep in.

LANGUAGE: LANGUAGE EXPRESSION

● **Lesson 5: Paragraphs (cont.)**

Read the story below. Use it to answer questions 7–10.

(1) The beginning of the twentieth century brought the first real innovations in roller coasters. (2) American John Miller introduced banked tracks. (3) His inventions also included the safety devices that kept cars from rolling back while climbing a hill. (4) The cars could climb, and the popularity of the coasters climbed, too. (5) Then the Great Depression brought economic problems. (6) Scrap wood and metal were needed during World War II. (7) These two periods saw the closing of many parks and the dismantling of many coasters. (8) Afterwards, the popularity of the coasters rebounded as more new developments made them even exciting.

7. **Which sentence could be added after sentence 8?**

   Ⓐ Passengers were catapulted at speeds of up to 100 miles per hour.

   Ⓑ Theme parks today battle each other for the tallest, wildest and fastest rides.

   Ⓒ Roller coasters are very scary.

   Ⓓ The Wild Thriller is a new kind of coaster.

8. **What is the topic sentence of this paragraph?**

   Ⓕ 1

   Ⓖ 2

   Ⓗ 3

   Ⓙ 4

9. **Which sentence best combines sentences 5 and 6?**

   Ⓐ The Great Depression brought economic problems, and World War II a need for scrap wood and metal.

   Ⓑ Scrap wood was needed for World War II and the Great Depression brought economic problems.

   Ⓒ The Depression brought economic problems that caused World War II to need scrap wood and metal.

   Ⓓ Many economic problems caused a need for scrap wood and metal during the Great Depression.

10. **Which of the following sentences could be added after sentence 1?**

    Ⓕ At least one man can be credited with helping to make this happen.

    Ⓖ Coasters hang people from harnesses.

    Ⓗ He is afraid of coasters so he decided to invent safety features.

    Ⓙ She was plummeted 10 stories toward the ground.

STOP

Name _____ Date_____

LANGUAGE: LANGUAGE EXPRESSION
SAMPLE TEST

● **Directions:** Read the directions for each section. Select the best answer for each question.

Examples

Choose the word or phrase that best completes the sentence.

A. _____ at the mall during the earthquake?

- (A) Are you
- (B) Is you
- (C) Was you
- (D) Were you

Choose the answer that is a complete and correctly written sentence.

B.
- (F) I chopped lettuce for the salad.
- (G) Michelle slice the carrots and radishes.
- (H) Vicki brung a delicious salad dressing.
- (J) Marsha were late and brought chocolate chip cookies.

For numbers 1–3, choose the word or phrase that best completes the sentence.

1. **Our history teacher _____ a field trip for our class.**
   - (A) were planning
   - (B) is planned
   - (C) has planned
   - (D) has planning

2. **She _____ bees in a glass-walled hive in her backyard.**
   - (F) keeping
   - (G) were keeping
   - (H) did kept
   - (J) keeps

3. **Our everyday prices are _____ than our competitors' sale prices.**
   - (A) even lower
   - (B) even lowest
   - (C) even low
   - (D) more lower

For numbers 4–6, choose the answer that is a complete and correctly written sentence.

4.
- (F) People have been interest in birds since the beginning of time.
- (G) All birds doesn't fly.
- (H) Ostriches are the fastest birds on land.
- (J) Penguins, which have short body, use their wings like flippers.

5.
- (A) Last week, I couldn't find Rascal.
- (B) She is usually well behaved, and no dog are more loyal.
- (C) We did not discovered until two hours later that she disappeared.
- (D) I were so happy to find her!

6.
- (F) It are not easy to buy food when you are unemployed.
- (G) Many toddlers attending preschool before kindergarten.
- (H) It is a good idea to wore a life jacket while boating.
- (J) I was late for school because I forgot my umbrella.

GO ON

Name _____ Date _____

For numbers 7–11, read each answer choice. Fill in the space for the choice that has a usage error. If there is no mistake, fill in the fourth answer space.

7.
(A) Anthony is a very responsible person.
(B) He goes to school and visit his grandfather.
(C) Last year, his classmates gave him a birthday party.
(D) no mistakes

8.
(F) The weather caused the ball game to be postponed.
(G) We played the game on Saturday and lost.
(H) We still enjoyed a pizza party after it was all over.
(J) no mistakes

9.
(A) I really enjoying singing in the school choir with my girlfriend.
(B) My friend also knows how to play the piano.
(C) Someday I would like to learn to play an instrument.
(D) no mistakes

10.
(F) When you make up your mind about something, you are making a decision.
(G) Sometimes making a decision can seem like a difficult thing to do.
(H) It feels good to make a right decision.
(J) no mistakes

11.
(A) After landing, what was the first thing you saw from your spaceship?
(B) Did you seen that strange creature standing by the tree?
(C) Many people enjoy the journey to our planet.
(D) no mistakes

For numbers 12–15, choose the best way to write the underlined part of each sentence. If the underlined part is correct, fill in the fourth answer space.

12. You've likely heard of the Wright brothers and their contribution to aviation.
(F) his contribution
(G) they contributed
(H) their contributes
(J) no change

13. A telescope are a tool to look at things that are far away.
(A) was a tool
(B) is a tool
(C) were a tool
(D) no change

14. A reporter found out information and then carries it back to other people.
(F) finds out
(G) find out
(H) do finds
(J) no change

GO ON

15. A microphone magnifies your voice so that people far away <u>can hear</u> you.

- (A) can't hear
- (B) can heard
- (C) can hearing
- (D) no change

Read the story below. Use it to answer the questions.

(1) What lives in the ocean and can give you four hugs at once? (2) It is an octopus, of course. (3) Many people think that <u>octopuses are</u> fierce animals, but they are really quite shy. (4) When an enemy is near, an octopus may protect itself in a number of ways. (5) It may hide by changing its color to <u>match it is</u> surroundings. (6) It can even turn two colors at once to <u>confuses its enemy</u>. (7) Or it may squeeze its soft body between two rocks so it won't be noticed. (8) If an enemy does spot it, the octopus can swim away by shooting water <u>throughout a tube</u> on its body. (9) It can also send a liquid that looks like ink through the tube. (10) The liquid makes a black cloud that hides the octopus and confuses the enemy.

16. In sentence 3, <u>octopuses are</u> is best written—

- (F) octopuses is
- (G) octopus' are
- (H) octopuses was
- (J) no change

17. In sentence 5, <u>match it is</u> is best written—

- (A) matched its
- (B) matching its
- (C) match its
- (D) no change

18. In sentence 6, <u>confuses its enemy</u> is best written—

- (F) confuse its enemy
- (G) confused its enemy
- (H) confuse enemy
- (J) no change

19. In sentence 8, <u>throughout a tube</u> is best written—

- (A) before a tube
- (B) threw out a tube
- (C) through a tube
- (D) no change

For numbers 20–21, find the underlined part that is the simple subject of the sentence.

20. The (F) <u>morning's</u> (G) <u>thunderstorm</u> (H) <u>threatened</u> to close the (J) <u>fair</u>.

- (F) morning's
- (G) thunderstorm
- (H) threatened
- (J) fair

21. (A) <u>Many</u> (B) <u>dark</u> (C) <u>clouds</u> drifted across the (D) <u>sky</u>.

- (A) Many
- (B) dark
- (C) clouds
- (D) sky

GO ON

Name _____   Date _____

For numbers 22–23, find the underlined part that is the simple predicate of the sentence.

22. The fierce (F) storm (G) sent people (H) scurrying for (J) shelter.

   F storm
   G sent
   H scurrying
   J shelter

23. In less than an (A) hour's (B) time, the angry (C) storm (D) ended.

   A hour's
   B time
   C storm
   D ended

For numbers 24–27, choose the answer that best combines the underlined sentences.

24. The store is having a sale.
   The sale is week-long.

   F The week-long sale was had by the store.
   G The store is having a sale that is week-long.
   H The sale that is week-long is at the store.
   J The store is having a week-long sale.

25. We ate fish for dinner.
   We ate at the new restaurant.

   A We ate fish for dinner at the new restaurant.
   B We ate fish at the restaurant.
   C The restaurant served fish for dinner.
   D At the new restaurant we ate fish for dinner.

26. Many children's books have colorful pictures.
   Many children's books have large pictures.
   Many children's books have few words.

   F Many children's books have colorful pictures and few words.
   G Many children's books have large, colorful pictures.
   H Many children's books have large, colorful pictures and few words.
   J Children's books have many words and large, colorful pictures.

27. The sheep's wool will be sheared.
   The farmer will shear the sheep.
   The sheep will be sheared tomorrow.

   A The sheep's wool will be sheared tomorrow by the farmer.
   B The sheep's wool will be sheared tomorrow.
   C The farmer will shear the sheep's wool tomorrow.
   D Tomorrow, the farmer will shear the wool from the sheep.

GO ON

LANGUAGE: LANGUAGE EXPRESSION
SAMPLE TEST (cont.)

Read the paragraphs below. Find the best topic sentence for each paragraph.

28. _____. It keeps your mind working well. Everyone should do some mental exercises everyday. These kinds of exercises help you think clearly. They help you solve problems quickly and easily.

　　(F) You can write a poem or do mathematics.

　　(G) They help you understand your feelings better.

　　(H) The mind should not be wasted.

　　(J) Mental exercise helps improve your mind.

29. _____. Wolf puppies grow into 150 pound wild animals that are difficult to control and train. People with wolf puppies are soon faced with a huge dilemma. What's worse, these wolves can't be returned to the wild because they have not learned to hunt for themselves.

　　(A) Wolf puppies have soft fur.

　　(B) Wild animals can be frightening.

　　(C) Although wolf puppies are cute, they do not make good pets.

　　(D) Private groups across the country adopt wolves.

30. _____. Most sea otters live near the North Pacific Ocean. They have hind feet shaped like flippers that allow them to swim easily on their backs. Sea otters even float on their backs while they eat, sleep, and carry their babies. They can also stay under water longer than most other mammals—almost four minutes!

　　(F) The sea otter is a fascinating mammal.

　　(G) This helps them hunt for food such as clams, crabs, fish, and squid.

　　(H) Mammals are interesting creatures.

　　(J) Sea otters are adorable.

31. _____. The black box keeps track of information during a flight. It records how fast the plane is flying and how high it is above the ground. It also records information about the equipment and the actions of the pilots. When a plane crashes, investigators use it to find out what went wrong.

　　(A) Flying in an airplane is the best way to travel to distant destinations.

　　(B) Black boxes are not necessarily black.

　　(C) Pilots use complicated navigation equipment when flying a plane.

　　(D) Airplanes usually carry a device called a flight data recorder, or a *black box*.

STOP

LANGUAGE: SPELLING

● Lesson 6: Spelling

Directions: Follow the directions for each section. Choose the answer you think is correct.

⎛ **Examples** ⎞

Find the word that is spelled correctly and fits best in the sentence.

A. If we _____, we will win.

- Ⓐ coperate
- Ⓑ cooperate
- Ⓒ coopperate
- Ⓓ coopirate

Choose the phrase in which the underlined word is not spelled correctly.

B.
- Ⓕ brave soldier
- Ⓖ <u>victorious</u> team
- Ⓗ <u>selebrate</u> a holiday
- Ⓙ unusual <u>circumstances</u>

 Clue Read the directions carefully. Be sure you know if you should look for the correctly spelled word or the incorrectly spelled word.

● Practice

For numbers 1–6, choose the word that is spelled correctly and best completes the sentence.

1. A good scientist knows how to _____ natural events.

- Ⓐ obsirve
- Ⓑ obzerve
- Ⓒ obscirve
- Ⓓ observe

2. Tim made an _____ to his bicycle.

- Ⓕ adjustment
- Ⓖ ajustment
- Ⓗ ajustmint
- Ⓙ adjustmine

3. The new business made the town _____.

- Ⓐ prosperous
- Ⓑ prosprous
- Ⓒ prosperus
- Ⓓ prospirous

4. The weather is _____ here.

- Ⓕ changiable
- Ⓖ changeuble
- Ⓗ changeable
- Ⓙ changable

5. Sugar _____ in hot liquid.

- Ⓐ dissolves
- Ⓑ disolves
- Ⓒ discolves
- Ⓓ dissolfs

6. Trees blew over during the _____.

- Ⓕ hurrycane
- Ⓖ hurricane
- Ⓗ huricane
- Ⓙ hurrikane

GO ON

● Lesson 6: Spelling (cont.)

For numbers 7–14, choose the phrase in which the underlined word is not spelled correctly.

7. (A) create a <u>budget</u>
    (B) castle <u>guardian</u>
    (C) <u>legendary</u> explorer
    (D) <u>advertized</u> price

8. (F) <u>comfortable</u> shoes
    (G) cool <u>celer</u>
    (H) <u>mentioned</u> a name
    (J) dangerous <u>expedition</u>

9. (A) <u>spesific</u> information
    (B) <u>census</u> taker
    (C) my <u>niece</u>
    (D) gift <u>certificate</u>

10. (F) <u>sacrifice</u> quality
    (G) <u>circular</u> saw
    (H) <u>fierce</u> storm
    (J) four <u>cilinder</u>

11. (A) <u>discard</u> the report
    (B) <u>oragin</u> of man
    (C) <u>guitar</u> player
    (D) strong <u>fortress</u>

12. (F) magic <u>formulla</u>
    (G) late <u>departure</u>
    (H) <u>ordinary</u> day
    (J) pretty <u>ornament</u>

13. (A) <u>nonprofit</u> group
    (B) <u>independent</u> thinking
    (C) <u>encorrect</u> thinking
    (D) high <u>humidity</u>

14. (F) heavy <u>equipment</u>
    (G) <u>fraction</u> of an inch
    (H) good <u>dispositian</u>
    (J) bad <u>decision</u>

STOP

Name _____   Date _____

● **Directions:** Follow the directions for each section. Choose the answer you think is correct.

Examples

Find the word that is spelled correctly and fits best in the sentence.

A. Let's buy a hot dog at the _____ stand.

- Ⓐ consecion
- Ⓑ concesion
- Ⓒ concession
- Ⓓ concetion

Choose the phrase in which the underlined word is not spelled correctly.

B.
- Ⓕ absorption rate
- Ⓖ long distence running
- Ⓗ have patience
- Ⓙ a little annoyance

For numbers 1–6, choose the word that is spelled correctly and best completes the sentence.

1. The child needed a little more _____.

- Ⓐ guidance
- Ⓑ gidence
- Ⓒ guidince
- Ⓓ guidence

2. Joylyn enjoyed the _____ of the movie.

- Ⓕ prevew
- Ⓖ preeview
- Ⓗ preview
- Ⓙ prevue

3. The _____ for the meeting went quickly.

- Ⓐ preperation
- Ⓑ preparasion
- Ⓒ prepparation
- Ⓓ preparation

4. Take extra _____ and lock the doors.

- Ⓕ precaution
- Ⓖ precausion
- Ⓗ precaushon
- Ⓙ precawtion

5. I do not mean to _____ on you.

- Ⓐ inpose
- Ⓑ impos
- Ⓒ impose
- Ⓓ impoes

6. Sara did not _____ the tire on her bicycle.

- Ⓕ inflat
- Ⓖ inflait
- Ⓗ imflate
- Ⓙ inflate

GO ON

Name _____ Date _____

For numbers 7–14, choose the phrase in which the underlined word is not spelled correctly.

7.
- (A) wonderful dessert
- (B) incredible journey
- (C) outstandig job
- (D) miraculous recovery

8.
- (F) champian boxer
- (G) community college
- (H) rock collection
- (J) compound fracture

9.
- (A) concentrate hard
- (B) suburban home
- (C) submurge the submarine
- (D) captive audience

10.
- (F) aggressive treatment
- (G) heart was deffective
- (H) new red tricycle
- (J) mysterious unicorn

11.
- (A) triplicate copies
- (B) voice was monotone
- (C) biannual report
- (D) sing in unisun.

12.
- (F) yact club
- (G) terrible cough
- (H) sharp scissors
- (J) fish aquarium

13.
- (A) civil war
- (B) baby daghter
- (C) dance a waltz
- (D) awkward move

14.
- (F) plant almanac
- (G) haughty laugh
- (H) applaud loudly
- (J) alternat rows

STOP

Name _____   Date_____

LANGUAGE: STUDY SKILLS

● Lesson 7: Study Skills

Directions: Follow the directions for each section. Choose the answer you think is correct.

Examples

A. If you want to find out the correct spelling of a word you would use a—

- (A) dictionary
- (B) almanac
- (C) glossary
- (D) thesaurus

B. In which of these books would you find information about twentieth century art?

- (F) *Art of the Egyptian Pyramids*
- (G) *Baroque Architecture*
- (H) *Famous Artists of the 20th Century*
- (J) *Cave Paintings*

 Clue Read the directions carefully. Refer back to any tables to help you find the correct answers.

● Practice

Use this table of contents to answer questions 1–3.

TABLE OF CONTENTS

Chapter 1: Nature of Matter 5
Chapter 2: Light 21
Chapter 3: Sound 34
Chapter 4: Simple Machines 41
Chapter 5: Magnetism 52
Chapter 6: Static Electricity 60
Chapter 7: Current Electricity 68

1. In which chapter would you find information on how sound travels?

- (A) Chapter 3
- (B) Chapter 2
- (C) Chapter 5
- (D) Chapter 7

2. Where would you find information on prisms?

- (F) between pages 25 and 40
- (G) between pages 33 and 34
- (H) between pages 21 and 33
- (J) between pages 60 and 68

3. In which chapter would you find information on circuits?

- (A) Chapter 1
- (B) Chapter 5
- (C) Chapter 6
- (D) Chapter 7

Choose the best answer for numbers 4–6.

4. Which of these would you find in a thesaurus?

- (F) a synonym for the word *merry*
- (G) information on the Gettysburg Address
- (H) the distance from the earth to the moon
- (J) a list of children's book authors

GO ON

Name _____ Date _____

LANGUAGE: STUDY SKILLS

● **Lesson 7: Study Skills (cont.)**

The Dewey Decimal System is used in libraries to categorize nonfiction books. Use the summary of this system to answer numbers 5–8.

000–099	Generalities (encyclopedias, periodicals)
100–199	Philosophy and Related Disciplines
200–299	Religion
300–399	Social Sciences (law, government)
400–499	Language
500–599	Pure Sciences (math, chemistry)
600–699	Technology
700–799	The Arts and Recreation
800–899	Literature
900–999	Geography and History

5. **Which of these books would probably be found in category 600–699?**
    (A) Setting up Your PC System
    (B) Using Mathematical Formulas
    (C) How to Draw Portraits
    (D) The Great Western Migration

6. **In which category would a book about gold be found?**
    (F) 300–399
    (G) 500–599
    (H) 600–699
    (J) 700–799

7. **The information in parentheses shows just a few of the topics that are found under the main headings. Which of these topics might also be found under "Social Sciences"?**
    (A) automobiles
    (B) needlepoint
    (C) electricity
    (D) electoral votes

8. **Where would you find a book about speech patterns?**
    (F) 200–299
    (G) 500–599
    (H) 400–499
    (J) 700–799

Read each question below. Select the correct answer.

9. **Look at these guide words from a dictionary page.**

    Which word would be found on the page?
    (A) nosegay
    (B) novel
    (C) notch
    (D) nozzle

guide words
nothing–now

10. **Look at these guide words from a dictionary page.**

    Which word would not be found on the page?
    (F) sample
    (G) sanction
    (H) sand
    (J) sandwich

guide words
same–sandal

GO ON

1-57768-977-1 — *Spectrum Test Practice 7*

LANGUAGE: STUDY SKILLS

● Lesson 7: Study Skills (cont.)

Use the index below to answer questions 11–14. The index is from a resource about owning a business.

Index

processors, word, 154
product
      business, definition of a, 33
      liability insurance, 132
      mix, in marketing, 37,67
      in sample business plan, 266
      and service analysis, in a business
           plan,170–171, 261, 266
productivity, increasing, 185
professional liability insurance, 132
profile
      customer, 80
      management, 173–174
profit, 41
      calculation of, 99
      definition of, on income statement, 97
      margin, calculation of, 60–61
      sharing, 194
      test, 183
programs, graphics for business uses, 164
records, employee, 118–119
recruitment ads, 188–189
relations, customer, 92–93
research
      firms, types of, 45–46
retirement plans, 194–195
sales
      programs, 12
      techniques, 13
sales volume, estimating, 74–75
software
      business planning, 179
      computer, 163–165

11. On which pages would you find information about companies that could help you do research?
    (A) 45–46
    (B) 60–61
    (C) 188–189
    (D) 74–75

12. On pages 12–13, you will not find what information?
    (F) sales programs
    (G) sales techniques
    (H) calling potential customers
    (J) how to balance the budget

13. From looking at the index, what can you conclude about this resource?
    (A) You can find out how to fire an employee.
    (B) You can learn about liability insurance.
    (C) You can find out about research on the Internet.
    (D) You can find out about old record albums.

14. What can you find out on page 164?
    (F) about creating a business plan
    (G) about increasing productivity
    (H) about graphics programs
    (J) about profit margins

STOP

Name _____ Date_____

LANGUAGE: STUDY SKILLS
SAMPLE TEST

● **Directions:** Read each section carefully. Select the correct answers.

Examples

A. Which of the following would you go to for information on zebras?

- (A) dictionary
- (B) almanac
- (C) wildlife encyclopedia
- (D) newspaper

B. Which of these would you most likely find in the index of a book about camping?

- (F) Outdoor Publishing, California
- (G) restaurants, 30–41
- (H) backpacks, 12–14
- (J) Hawaii: beaches

For numbers 1–3, choose the word that would appear first if the words were arranged in alphabetical order.

1.
- (A) notify
- (B) notion
- (C) noun
- (D) nourish

2.
- (F) dome
- (G) domain
- (H) domestic
- (J) dominant

3.
- (A) tuft
- (B) tube
- (C) tuck
- (D) tub

For numbers 4–5, choose the answer that you think is correct.

4. Which of these books would be the best source of information for a report on the moon's surface?
- (F) *Our Solar System*
- (G) *The Earth's Moon*
- (H) *Known Moons of Jupiter*
- (J) *Build Your Own Rocket*

5. If you were writing a research report, you would list the books you used as references in the—
- (A) index
- (B) glossary
- (C) bibliography
- (D) table of contents

Name _____   Date _____

For numbers 6–9, choose the answer that you think is correct.

6. **The first place to look for a magazine article on healthy cooking would be—**

   (F) the *Reader's Guide to Periodical Literature*

   (G) a library index

   (H) an atlas

   (J) a weekend newspaper

7. **If you are in a bookstore and want a quick overview of what a book is about, you would look at the—**

   (A) index

   (B) glossary

   (C) table of contents

   (D) bibliography

8. **If you wanted to know when a book was published, you would look at the—**

   (F) title page

   (G) copyright page

   (H) front cover

   (J) index

9. **If you wanted to know who the author of a book wanted to thank for their contributions, you would look at the—**

   (A) bibliography

   (B) title page

   (C) introduction

   (D) acknowledgments page

The Dewey Decimal System is used in libraries to categorize nonfiction books. Use the summary of this system to answer numbers 10–11.

000–099	Generalities (encyclopedias, periodicals)
100–199	Philosophy and Related Disciplines
200–299	Religion
300–399	Social Sciences (law, government)
400–499	Language
500–599	Pure Sciences (math, chemistry)
600–699	Technology
700–799	The Arts and Recreation
800–899	Literature
900–999	Geography and History

10. **Where would a book about the metamorphosis of a butterfly be found?**

    (F) 500–599

    (G) 600–699

    (H) 800–899

    (J) 900–999

11. **If you were doing a research paper on the various landforms found in the United States, you would look in—**

    (A) Geography and History

    (B) Technology

    (C) Social Sciences

    (D) Pure Sciences

STOP

ANSWER SHEET

Part 1: LANGUAGE MECHANICS

A Ⓐ Ⓑ Ⓒ Ⓓ   6 Ⓕ Ⓖ Ⓗ Ⓙ   13 Ⓐ Ⓑ Ⓒ Ⓓ
B Ⓕ Ⓖ Ⓗ Ⓙ   7 Ⓐ Ⓑ Ⓒ Ⓓ   14 Ⓕ Ⓖ Ⓗ Ⓙ
1 Ⓐ Ⓑ Ⓒ Ⓓ   8 Ⓕ Ⓖ Ⓗ Ⓙ   15 Ⓐ Ⓑ Ⓒ Ⓓ
2 Ⓕ Ⓖ Ⓗ Ⓙ   9 Ⓐ Ⓑ Ⓒ Ⓓ
3 Ⓐ Ⓑ Ⓒ Ⓓ   10 Ⓕ Ⓖ Ⓗ Ⓙ
4 Ⓕ Ⓖ Ⓗ Ⓙ   11 Ⓐ Ⓑ Ⓒ Ⓓ
5 Ⓐ Ⓑ Ⓒ Ⓓ   12 Ⓕ Ⓖ Ⓗ Ⓙ

Part 2: LANGUAGE EXPRESSION

A Ⓐ Ⓑ Ⓒ Ⓓ   10 Ⓕ Ⓖ Ⓗ Ⓙ   21 Ⓐ Ⓑ Ⓒ Ⓓ
B Ⓕ Ⓖ Ⓗ Ⓙ   11 Ⓐ Ⓑ Ⓒ Ⓓ   22 Ⓕ Ⓖ Ⓗ Ⓙ
1 Ⓐ Ⓑ Ⓒ Ⓓ   12 Ⓕ Ⓖ Ⓗ Ⓙ   23 Ⓐ Ⓑ Ⓒ Ⓓ
2 Ⓕ Ⓖ Ⓗ Ⓙ   13 Ⓐ Ⓑ Ⓒ Ⓓ   24 Ⓕ Ⓖ Ⓗ Ⓙ
3 Ⓐ Ⓑ Ⓒ Ⓓ   14 Ⓕ Ⓖ Ⓗ Ⓙ   25 Ⓐ Ⓑ Ⓒ Ⓓ
4 Ⓕ Ⓖ Ⓗ Ⓙ   15 Ⓐ Ⓑ Ⓒ Ⓓ
5 Ⓐ Ⓑ Ⓒ Ⓓ   16 Ⓕ Ⓖ Ⓗ Ⓙ
6 Ⓕ Ⓖ Ⓗ Ⓙ   17 Ⓐ Ⓑ Ⓒ Ⓓ
7 Ⓐ Ⓑ Ⓒ Ⓓ   18 Ⓕ Ⓖ Ⓗ Ⓙ
8 Ⓕ Ⓖ Ⓗ Ⓙ   19 Ⓐ Ⓑ Ⓒ Ⓓ
9 Ⓐ Ⓑ Ⓒ Ⓓ   20 Ⓕ Ⓖ Ⓗ Ⓙ

Part 3: SPELLING

A Ⓐ Ⓑ Ⓒ Ⓓ   6 Ⓕ Ⓖ Ⓗ Ⓙ   13 Ⓐ Ⓑ Ⓒ Ⓓ
B Ⓕ Ⓖ Ⓗ Ⓙ   7 Ⓐ Ⓑ Ⓒ Ⓓ   14 Ⓕ Ⓖ Ⓗ Ⓙ
1 Ⓐ Ⓑ Ⓒ Ⓓ   8 Ⓕ Ⓖ Ⓗ Ⓙ
2 Ⓕ Ⓖ Ⓗ Ⓙ   9 Ⓐ Ⓑ Ⓒ Ⓓ
3 Ⓐ Ⓑ Ⓒ Ⓓ   10 Ⓕ Ⓖ Ⓗ Ⓙ
4 Ⓕ Ⓖ Ⓗ Ⓙ   11 Ⓐ Ⓑ Ⓒ Ⓓ
5 Ⓐ Ⓑ Ⓒ Ⓓ   12 Ⓕ Ⓖ Ⓗ Ⓙ

Part 4: STUDY SKILLS

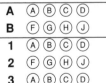

A Ⓐ Ⓑ Ⓒ Ⓓ   10 Ⓕ Ⓖ Ⓗ Ⓙ
B Ⓕ Ⓖ Ⓗ Ⓙ   11 Ⓐ Ⓑ Ⓒ Ⓓ
1 Ⓐ Ⓑ Ⓒ Ⓓ
2 Ⓕ Ⓖ Ⓗ Ⓙ
3 Ⓐ Ⓑ Ⓒ Ⓓ
4 Ⓕ Ⓖ Ⓗ Ⓙ
5 Ⓐ Ⓑ Ⓒ Ⓓ
6 Ⓕ Ⓖ Ⓗ Ⓙ
7 Ⓐ Ⓑ Ⓒ Ⓓ
8 Ⓕ Ⓖ Ⓗ Ⓙ
9 Ⓐ Ⓑ Ⓒ Ⓓ

Name _____   Date _____

LANGUAGE PRACTICE TEST

● Part 1: Language Mechanics

Directions: Read each item. Mark the space for the punctuation that is needed in the sentence. Mark the space for "None" if no more punctuation is needed.

Examples

A. "Don't worry about everything all at once, her grandmother told her.
- Ⓐ "
- Ⓑ '
- Ⓒ :
- Ⓓ None

B. Why is Tracy standing in line
- Ⓕ .
- Ⓖ ?
- Ⓗ !
- Ⓙ None

For numbers 1–7, read each item. Mark the space for the punctuation that is needed in the sentence. Mark the space for "None" if no more punctuation is needed.

1. Did you go to your best friends house?
- Ⓐ ,
- Ⓑ "
- Ⓒ '
- Ⓓ None

2. Enrique stood with one foot on the ground, the other on the pedal of his bicycle.
- Ⓕ ?
- Ⓖ :
- Ⓗ "
- Ⓙ None

3. The passage appeared in the December 8 1910, edition of the newspaper.
- Ⓐ ,
- Ⓑ :
- Ⓒ .
- Ⓓ None

4. He carefully examined the cows markings.
- Ⓕ ,
- Ⓖ "
- Ⓗ '
- Ⓙ None

5. Do not run in front of that car
- Ⓐ !
- Ⓑ .
- Ⓒ ?
- Ⓓ None

6. We visited my grandfather, brother, and Aunt Josie.
- Ⓕ ,
- Ⓖ "
- Ⓗ :
- Ⓙ None

7. At Food World we always hire friendly people-oriented individuals.
- Ⓐ "
- Ⓑ '
- Ⓒ ,
- Ⓓ None

GO ON

LANGUAGE PRACTICE TEST

Part 1: Language Mechanics (cont.)

For numbers 8–11, mark the space for the answer that shows the correct capitalization and punctuation.

8.
- (F) "Are you going to camp this summer," asked Mike.
- (G) "I signed up last week?" answered Pauline.
- (H) "I signed up too, responded Mike.
- (J) "Maybe we could go at the same time," suggested Pauline.

9.
- (A) Milk, cheese, and sour cream are products made from milk.
- (B) Oranges apples, and peaches grow on trees.
- (C) How often do you eat ice cream.
- (D) Eat more: fruit, vegetables, and whole grains.

10.
- (F) What musical instrument is for sale!
- (G) Sandras violin needs a new string.
- (H) Chandra learned to play the piano at the age of six.
- (J) "Let's go to the concert together, said Carolyn.

11.
- (A) You could spend many hours in a museum and not see everything.
- (B) An art museum, preserves and displays, works of art.
- (C) The largest one in the United States, the metropolitan museum of Art, includes over three million works of art.
- (D) An art museum carries' insurance to protect against loss and damage.

For numbers 12–15, mark the space for the correct capitalization and punctuation. Mark the space for "correct as it is" if the underlined part is correct.

12. **The lobster another favorite shellfish, has only five pairs of legs.**
- (F) lobster another, favorite
- (G) lobster, another favorite
- (H) lobster: another favorite
- (J) correct as it is

13. **Some museums have collections that cover only one subject such as dolls, airplanes, or antique toys.**
- (A) Dolls, Airplanes, or Antique Toys.
- (B) dolls airplanes or antique toys.
- (C) dolls, airplanes, or antique toys?
- (D) correct as it is

14. **At the Field Museum of natural history in Chicago you can learn about mummies.**
- (F) Natural History in chicago,
- (G) Natural History in Chicago,
- (H) Natural history in Chicago,
- (J) correct as it is

15. **There are so many kinds of museum's to visit, choosing only one could be a difficult decision.**
- (A) kinds of museums
- (B) kinds of museums,
- (C) kind's of museums
- (D) correct as it is

Name _____ Date _____

LANGUAGE PRACTICE TEST

● **Part 2: Language Expression**

Directions: Read the directions for each section. Select the best answer for each question.

Examples

Choose the word or phrase that best completes the sentence.

A. I _____ to the movie but was late anyway.

 (A) hurried
 (B) hurries
 (C) hurrying
 (D) hurry

Choose the answer that is a complete and correctly written sentence.

B.
 (F) You may has some dessert.
 (G) The farmer feed the sows and their piglets.
 (H) Valerie did went on a vacation.
 (J) Jessica sat on a park bench and fed a dove.

For numbers 1–3, choose the word or phrase that best completes the sentence.

1. **Hundreds of people _____ winter vacations there each year.**
 (A) had taken
 (B) has taken
 (C) were taken
 (D) had taking

2. **The hail, _____ fell like golf balls to the ground, damaged the car.**
 (F) where
 (G) who
 (H) which
 (J) what

3. **The hot air balloon _____ into the blue sky.**
 (A) risen
 (B) rises
 (C) raises
 (D) had raised

For numbers 4–6, choose the answer that is a complete and correctly written sentence

4.
 (F) The sound track began very strangely.
 (G) There was a suddenly surge of volume.
 (H) It is not the usually way for a film to begin.
 (J) The credits were extreme long.

5.
 (A) The drugstore in town are open today.
 (B) The musical with the best choreography weren't win.
 (C) The cottage beside the brook was sold last year.
 (D) The doctors in the hospital is working very hard.

6.
 (F) I haven't got no time to wait for you.
 (G) You don't know nothing about the subject.
 (H) You can't hardly find that tape anywhere.
 (J) Polly did not have

GO ON

For numbers 7–9, choose the answer that best combines the underlined sentences.

7. **The cat ran across the street.**
   The scared, yellow cat ran.
   - Ⓐ The scared cat ran across the yellow street.
   - Ⓑ The scared, yellow cat ran across the street.
   - Ⓒ The cat, which was scared and yellow, ran across the street.
   - Ⓓ The yellow cat ran across the street.

8. **Adella went to the restaurant.**
   Adella went to the movie.
   - Ⓕ Adella went to the movie and then she went to the restaurant.
   - Ⓖ The movie Adella went to was by the restaurant.
   - Ⓗ Adella went to the restaurant and the movie.
   - Ⓙ She went to the movie and then to the restaurant.

9. **Jerry finished reading his book. The book was about the Great Depression. The book was 125 pages.**
   - Ⓐ Jerry finished the book about the Great Depression and the book was 125 pages long.
   - Ⓑ Jerry's book about the Great Depression was 125 pages long.
   - Ⓒ Jerry finished reading the long book about the Depression.
   - Ⓓ Jerry finished reading his 125-page book about the Great Depression.

Read the paragraphs below. Find the best topic sentence for each paragraph.

10. _____. **His images could create a record of national life. When the Civil War broke out, he wanted to document the war. His efforts culminated in an 1862 display of photographs made after the Battle of Antietam. The photographs made an impression on those who saw them.**
    - Ⓕ Brady was a great photographer.
    - Ⓖ Photographers can learn from Brady.
    - Ⓗ The Civil War was a difficult war.
    - Ⓙ Brady thought that photography could serve an important purpose.

11. _____. **Some people like to eat cold pizza in the morning for breakfast. Others like to eat cereal or toast.**
    - Ⓐ All people should like pizza.
    - Ⓑ People like to eat different things.
    - Ⓒ The time of day influences what we eat.
    - Ⓓ Foods can be prepared in many ways.

GO ON

Find the answer choice that best develops the topic sentence below.

12. **The new nation needed a capitol building.**

   (F) Thomas Jefferson and George Washington decided to hold a competition for the best design.

   (G) The building would have grass around it.

   (H) George Washington is a symbol of the nation.

   (J) All countries should have their own capitol building.

Read the paragraph and answer questions 13–16.

(1) While approaching the airfield, pilot Mike Warren's two-seater plane was tossed by the wake of a departing aircraft. (2) He tried to regained control, but could not avoid the power lines. (3) One wheel caught, flipping the plane upside down. (4) It bounced on the power lines. (5) When the bouncing slowed, Warren was left dangling upside down, 60 feet above the ground. (6) Rescuers turned off the power before positioning two cranes beneath the plane. (7) After attached straps to stabilize the plane, they used a cherry picker to get close to Warren. (8) They unstrapped him from his seat belt and slowly brought him down. (9) Warren should have felt right at home. (10) His wife was relieved. (11) When he isn't flipping planes upside down, he works as a crane operator.

13. **How is sentence 2 best written?**

   (A) He tried to gain control, but avoided the power lines.

   (B) He tried to gaining control, but could not avoid the power lines.

   (C) He tried to regain control, but could not avoid the power lines.

   (D) He tried to gained control, but could not avoid the lines.

14. **In sentence 7, attached is best written—**

   (F) was attached

   (G) reattaching

   (H) attaching

   (J) as it is

15. **How could sentences 3 and 4 be combined without changing their meaning?**

   (A) One wheel caught, flipping the plane upside down, bouncing it on the power lines.

   (B) One wheel caught, flipping the plane and bouncing it on the power lines.

   (C) The plane was flipped and bounced on the power lines.

   (D) One wheel caught, and it made the plane bounce on the power lines.

16. **Which of these sentences does not belong in the report?**

   (F) 5

   (G) 8

   (H) 9

   (J) 10

GO ON

DISCIPLINE PRACTICE TEST

Part 2: Language Expression (cont.)

For numbers 17–21, read each answer choice. Fill in the space for the choice that has a usage error. If there is no mistake, fill in the fourth answer space.

17.
- Ⓐ At last week's luncheon
- Ⓑ for women in banking,
- Ⓒ pasta was served,
- Ⓓ no mistakes

18.
- Ⓕ Let's review the game
- Ⓖ to seen
- Ⓗ our mistakes.
- Ⓙ no mistakes

19.
- Ⓐ She little sister
- Ⓑ went to pre school
- Ⓒ before kindergarten.
- Ⓓ no mistakes

20.
- Ⓕ I'm tired of hearing
- Ⓖ him moan
- Ⓗ about he allowance.
- Ⓙ no mistakes

21.
- Ⓐ Our teacher told us
- Ⓑ to write a report about
- Ⓒ a famous person.
- Ⓓ no mistakes

For numbers 22–25, choose the best way to write the underlined part of each sentence. If the underlined part is correct, fill in the fourth answer space.

22. Research <u>is a method</u> of finding answers to questions.
- Ⓕ were a method
- Ⓖ is a methods
- Ⓗ are a method
- Ⓙ no change

23. The chapter at the end of my social studies book <u>is telling about</u> places.
- Ⓐ were telling about
- Ⓑ is told about
- Ⓒ tells about
- Ⓓ no change

24. The table of contents tells what <u>were contained</u> in a book.
- Ⓕ is contained
- Ⓖ is contain
- Ⓗ are contained
- Ⓙ no change

25. <u>It is important</u> to do original work and not copy the work of others.
- Ⓐ It are important
- Ⓑ It weren't important
- Ⓒ It were important
- Ⓓ no change

LANGUAGE PRACTICE TEST

● Part 3: Spelling

Directions: Follow the directions for each section. Choose the answer you think is correct.

Examples

Find the word that is spelled correctly and fits best in the sentence.

A.   He _____ a heavy-duty crane.

- (A) operats
- (B) operates
- (C) opperates
- (D) operaits

Choose the phrase in which the underlined word is not spelled correctly.

B.
- (F) tolerate bad behavior
- (G) bad temperament
- (H) chemical reactian
- (J) concert violinist

For numbers 1–6, choose the word that is spelled correctly and best completes the sentence.

1.   **Mary likes to _____ with her uncle.**
- (A) correspond
- (B) corespond
- (C) correspand
- (D) coresspond

2.   **You can purchase medicine at a _____.**
- (F) pharmacie
- (G) pharmicy
- (H) farmacy
- (J) pharmacy

3.   **Sandy _____ rocks.**
- (A) colects
- (B) collects
- (C) kolects
- (D) colleks

4.   **My mom and my aunt are _____ friends.**
- (F) cloce
- (G) klose
- (H) close
- (J) clos

5.   **There is _____ behind the door.**
- (A) moovement
- (B) movement
- (C) movemint
- (D) movemant

6.   **There is _____ in the next room.**
- (F) commotion
- (G) comotion
- (H) commosian
- (J) commoshon

GO ON

LANGUAGE PRACTICE TEST
Part 3: Spelling (Cont.)

For numbers 7–14, choose the phrase in which the underlined word is not spelled correctly.

7.
- (A) a pair of <u>oxen</u>
- (B) three <u>foxes</u>
- (C) little <u>elfs</u>
- (D) litter of <u>puppies</u>

8.
- (F) <u>delay</u> the event
- (G) <u>radio</u> program
- (H) baked <u>potato</u>
- (J) new born <u>caf</u>

9.
- (A) <u>foto</u> album
- (B) <u>mystery</u> theater
- (C) <u>review</u> the story
- (D) <u>retread</u> the tire

10.
- (F) <u>preschol</u> teacher
- (G) swim <u>underwater</u>
- (H) cold <u>compress</u>
- (J) <u>predict</u> the future

11.
- (A) <u>walk</u> slowly
- (B) <u>yell</u> loudly
- (C) <u>miniature</u> village
- (D) <u>prudint</u> judgement

12.
- (F) <u>justice</u> is served
- (G) <u>roar</u> loudly
- (H) <u>copy</u> machine
- (J) <u>tinie</u> creature

13.
- (A) <u>computer</u> monitor
- (B) <u>nationel</u> news
- (C) <u>political</u> science
- (D) wrote a <u>column</u>

14.
- (F) <u>glossary</u> of terms
- (G) scientific <u>theory</u>
- (H) secret <u>dokument</u>
- (J) <u>fiction</u> story

STOP

LANGUAGE PRACTICE TEST

● Part 4: Study Skills

Directions: Read each section carefully. Select the correct answers.

Examples

A. Which part of a book would you consult to find a definition of a word you do not know?

- (A) introduction
- (B) bibliography
- (C) glossary
- (D) copyright page

B. Which of these would you most likely find in the index of a book about mountain biking?

- (F) tire, fixing a flat, 32–34
- (G) Techniques for Hills, 41–43
- (H) Mountaineering Press, Colorado
- (J) swimming, 12–13

For numbers 1–3, choose the word that would appear first if the words were arranged in alphabetical order.

1.
   - (A) decoration
   - (B) decoy
   - (C) dedicate
   - (D) decree

2.
   - (F) huddle
   - (G) hover
   - (H) house
   - (J) hue

3.
   - (A) timber
   - (B) tile
   - (C) time
   - (D) tiger

For numbers 4–5, choose the answer that you think is correct.

4. Which of these books might be a source of information if you wanted to make ice cream?

   - (F) *The Complete Book of Cooking Outdoors*
   - (G) *A History of Machines*
   - (H) *Cool and Creamy Desserts*
   - (J) *Guide to Purchasing a Refrigerator*

5. If you were writing a research report, you would list your research resources in the—

   - (A) index.
   - (B) glossary.
   - (C) bibliography.
   - (D) table of contents.

GO ON

For numbers 6–8, choose the answer that you think is correct.

6. **How is this list of words organized?**
   dogs
   cats
   hamsters
   fish
   - (F) zoo animals
   - (G) aquarium animals
   - (H) household pets
   - (J) wild animals

7. **How is this list of words organized?**
   heart
   artery
   vein
   blood
   - (A) digestive system
   - (B) respiratory system
   - (C) skeletal system
   - (D) circulatory system

8. **Look at these guide words from a dictionary page. Which word would not be on this page?**
   - (F) nurse
   - (G) nutmeg
   - (H) nurture
   - (J) nylon

guide words
numerous–nuts

Use the index at the right to answer questions 9–11. The index is from a resource about works of art.

9. **How is an index in a book organized?**
   - (A) by subject
   - (B) alphabetical order
   - (C) by page numbers
   - (D) by interest of the reader

10. **On which pages would you look for information on natural-hair brushes?**
    - (F) 46 and 17
    - (G) 53 and 56
    - (H) 104 and 106
    - (J) 46 and 30

11. **Which information would you not be able to find in this book based on the index?**
    - (A) information about brushes
    - (B) information about abstract thinking
    - (C) information about conceptual art
    - (D) information about comic strips

Index
abstract art, 328–330
abstract expressionism, 436–444
Academy, French, 104
  founded, 104
  teaching under, 106
  finishing techniques, 107
brushes
  badger-hair, 46
  blending, 44
  fan, 84
  flat, 17, 88
  sable, 30
chalk
  ground, 56
  sketches, 53
comic strip
  in collage, 478
  influence of, 520
conceptual art, 493–496
conceptualism, 446

87

MATH: MATH CONCEPTS

● **Lesson 1: Numeration**

Directions: Read and work each problem. Find the correct answer.

Examples

A. Which of these numbers is a common multiple of 4, 6, and 8?

- (A) 22
- (B) 24
- (C) 32
- (D) 18

B. Which of these is smaller than ⁻6

- (F) 4
- (G) ⁻4
- (H) ⁻8
- (J) 0

 Clue Read each question carefully.

● **Practice**

1. Which point is at $\frac{1}{2}$ on this number line?

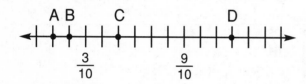

- (A) A
- (B) B
- (C) C
- (D) D

2. What number is expressed by $(3 \times 10^3) + (4 \times 10^2) + (8 \times 10^1)$

- (F) 3,408
- (G) 3,480
- (H) 34,800
- (J) 340,800

3. $\sqrt{144} =$

- (A) 9
- (B) 10
- (C) 11
- (D) 12

4. Which of these is another way to write the number in the box?

$$42,000,000 + 600,000 + 40 + 8$$

- (F) 42,600,048
- (G) 42,640,008
- (H) 43,640,080
- (J) 42,064,800

 GO ON

MATH: MATH CONCEPTS

● Lesson 1: Numeration (cont.)

5. What is the prime factorization of 64?
- (A) 8 x 8
- (B) 2 x 2 x 2 x 2 x 2 x 2
- (C) 2 x 32
- (D) 2 x 2 x 2 x 8

6. Which of these is less than 11^2?
- (F) 122
- (G) 112
- (H) 132
- (J) 142

7. What is the value of the expression in the box?

$$12 - 4 \times 6 =$$

- (A) 8
- (B) ⁻9
- (C) ⁻12
- (D) 0

8. Which of these is between 0.02 and 0.2 in value?
- (F) 0.2
- (G) 0.008
- (H) 0.6
- (J) 0.06

9. Which of these is another name for 8^3?
- (A) 8 x 3
- (B) 3 x 3 x 3 x 3 x 3 x 3 x 3 x 3
- (C) 8 x 8 x 8
- (D) 3

10. $6.2 \times 10^3 =$
- (F) 620
- (G) 6,200
- (H) 62,000
- (J) 620,000

11. What is the *smallest* number that can be divided evenly by 8 and 16?
- (A) 16
- (B) 128
- (C) 32
- (D) 24

12. ⁻7 + 9 =
- (F) ⁻4
- (G) 2
- (H) 16
- (J) ⁻2

GO ON

MATH: MATH CONCEPTS

● Lesson 1: Numeration (cont.)

13. Which of these is the greatest common factor of 32 and 72?

- (A) 3
- (B) 12
- (C) 9
- (D) 8

14. How much must you add to ⁻8 to get a number greater than 12?

- (F) a number between ⁻4 and 14
- (G) a number less than 5
- (H) a number less than ⁻4
- (J) a number greater than 20

15. Which number is greater than 42,648 but less than 53,229?

- (A) 42,528
- (B) 41,872
- (C) 53,326
- (D) 48,269

16. Which number is 462 rounded to the nearest tenth?

- (F) 460
- (G) 465
- (H) 400
- (J) 500

17. Which number is 8,219 rounded to the nearest hundred?

- (A) 8,220
- (B) 8,000
- (C) 8,300
- (D) 8,200

Use the following double bar graph to answer questions 18–19.

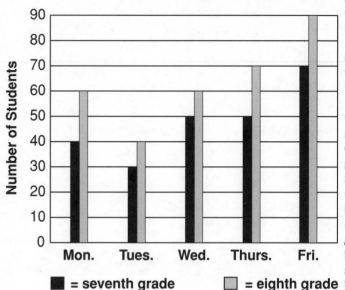

Hot Lunch Consumption

■ = seventh grade   ▥ = eighth grade

18. On which day do the most students buy lunch?

- (F) Tuesday
- (G) Friday
- (H) Monday
- (J) Wednesday

19. How many total lunches are purchased on Tuesday and Thursday?

- (A) 120
- (B) 80
- (C) 190
- (D) 200

STOP

Name _____ Date_____

MATH: MATH CONCEPTS

● **Lesson 2: Number Concepts**

Directions: Read and work each problem. Find the correct answer.

Examples

A. How would you read 9.6?

Ⓐ nine and six tenths

Ⓑ ninety six

Ⓒ nine and six hundredths

Ⓓ nine hundred and six

B. Which of these is a composite number?

Ⓕ 3

Ⓖ 19

Ⓗ 5

Ⓙ 24

 Key words, numbers, pictures, and figures will help you find the answers.

● **Practice**

1. 10,435 + 13,456 =

Ⓐ 12,000

Ⓑ 23,891

Ⓒ 22,000

Ⓓ 24,635

2. **Which describes the underlined portion in the numeral 21,6_4_8,362?**

Ⓕ thousands

Ⓖ tens of thousands

Ⓗ hundreds of thousands

Ⓙ millions

3. **What number goes in the blank to make the number sentence true?**

3 x (1 + 6) = (3 x 1) + (__ x 6)

Ⓐ 3

Ⓑ 0

Ⓒ 6

Ⓓ 1

4. **What is 0.89 rounded to the nearest tenth?**

Ⓕ 0.089

Ⓖ 0.85

Ⓗ 0.80

Ⓙ 0.9

GO ON ▶

● **Lesson 2: Number Concepts (cont.)**

5. Which of these is a prime number?
- (A) 27
- (B) 37
- (C) 21
- (D) 35

6. What number completes this number sentence?

6 x 20 = 10 x _____
- (F) 6
- (G) 12
- (H) 16
- (J) 60

7. Which of these is another way to write the number shown in the box?

500 + 40 + 0.3 + 0.01
- (A) 540.13
- (B) 543.10
- (C) 54.31
- (D) 540.31

8. Look carefully at the number pattern below. Which of these number sentences could be used to find the number that is missing from the number pattern?

2, 4, 6, 8, 10, 12, 14, _____, 18
- (F) 14 + 4 = 18
- (G) 18 − 4 = 14
- (H) 14 + 2 = 16
- (J) 16 + 2 = 18

9. 3,245 − 2,678 =
- (A) 267
- (B) 432
- (C) 567
- (D) 523

10. How much would the value of 624,008 be decreased by changing the 6 to a 5?
- (F) 24,000
- (G) 10,000
- (H) 100,000
- (J) 60,000

11. Ten million, two hundred six =
- (A) 10,000,206
- (B) 10,206,000
- (C) 10,026,000
- (D) 1,260,000

12. Look at the group of numbers in the box. Which statement about the numbers is true?

5, 7, 13, 17, 25
- (F) All of them are prime numbers.
- (G) None of the numbers are odd.
- (H) All of the numbers are even.
- (J) None of the numbers can be divided evenly by 4.

MATH: MATH CONCEPTS

● Lesson 2: Number Concepts (cont.)

13. What is the median of these numbers?

79 95 65 88 72

(A) 79
(B) 65
(C) 88
(D) 72

14. What is the average of these numbers?

6 24 32 15 18

(F) 24
(G) 95
(H) 19
(J) 32

15. What is 230.7 in expanded form?

(A) 2000 + 30 + 70
(B) 200 + 3 + 7.0
(C) 200 + 3 + 70
(D) 200 + 30 + 0.7

16. 28 − (3 + 6) x 3 =

(F) 57
(G) 18
(H) 1
(J) 3

17. What would be an appropriate integer to describe a $10.00 reduction?

(A) ⁻1
(B) ⁻10
(C) 10
(D) ⁻11

18. How would you write 4,800 in scientific notation?

(F) 4.8×10^3
(G) 48×10
(H) 48×10^3
(J) 4.8×10^2

19. What is the rule for the following pattern?

$$\frac{6}{3} \quad \frac{9}{4.5} \quad \frac{12}{6} \quad \frac{20}{10} \quad \frac{50}{25}$$

(A) denominator is twice the numerator
(B) numerators increase by threes
(C) the numbers increase
(D) numerator is twice the denominator

20. 34,654 + 3,768 =

(F) 39,456
(G) 37,986
(H) 38,422
(J) 38,232

STOP

Name _____   Date_____

MATH: MATH CONCEPTS

● Lesson 3: Fractions and Decimals

Directions: Read and work each problem. Find the correct answer.

A. Which fraction shows how many of the shapes on the right are shaded?

Ⓐ $\frac{1}{3}$

Ⓑ $\frac{2}{5}$

Ⓒ $\frac{1}{2}$

Ⓓ $\frac{3}{5}$

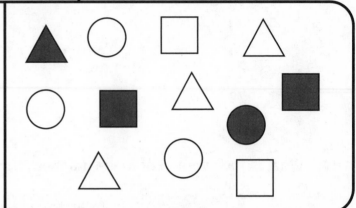

 Read each problem carefully, If you are not certain of the answer, come back to it later.

● Practice

1. 0.52 =

Ⓐ $\frac{52}{10}$

Ⓑ $\frac{52}{1}$

Ⓒ $\frac{52}{100}$

Ⓓ $\frac{52}{1000}$

2. Which number tells how much of the figure is shaded?

Ⓕ 0.20

Ⓖ 0.75

Ⓗ 0.50

Ⓙ 0.85

3. Which of these numbers comes between 8.25 and 8.37?

Ⓐ 7.99

Ⓑ 8.26

Ⓒ 8.42

Ⓓ 8.38

4. The fraction $\frac{25}{125}$ can be written as—

Ⓕ $\frac{1}{5}$

Ⓖ $\frac{1}{25}$

Ⓗ 5

Ⓙ $\frac{25}{100}$

GO ON

1-57768-977-1 — Spectrum Test Practice 7

MATH: MATH CONCEPTS

● **Lesson 3: Fractions and Decimals (cont.)**

5. **Two and eight ten-thousandths is equal to—**
   - (A) 2.08
   - (B) 2.008
   - (C) 2.8
   - (D) 2.0008

6. **What is 19.04 written in words?**
   - (F) nineteen and four hundredths
   - (G) nineteen and four tenths
   - (H) nineteen and ten fourths
   - (J) nineteen and four thousandths

7. **Which number represents the total proportion of unshaded figures?**
   - (A) $\frac{1}{2}$
   - (B) $\frac{7}{16}$
   - (C) $\frac{8}{16}$
   - (D) $\frac{1}{4}$

8. **2.68 =**
   - (F) $2\frac{68}{100}$
   - (G) $2\frac{68}{10}$
   - (H) $2\frac{68}{1000}$
   - (J) $\frac{2.68}{100}$

9. **Which of these numbers is less than 10.15?**
   - (A) 10.155
   - (B) 10.150
   - (C) 10.015
   - (D) 10.165

10. **$5\frac{1}{6}$ is equivalent to—**
    - (F) 31
    - (G) $\frac{31}{6}$
    - (H) $\frac{31}{5}$
    - (J) 5.6

11. **What is the missing number?**
    $$\frac{9}{11} = \frac{\square}{88}$$
    - (A) 62
    - (B) 11
    - (C) 99
    - (D) 72

GO ON

● **Lesson 3: Fractions and Decimals (cont.)**

12. **Which is the improper fraction for $7\frac{2}{3}$?**

    F) $\frac{23}{3}$

    G) $\frac{23}{7}$

    H) $7\frac{3}{2}$

    J) $\frac{23}{2}$

13. **What is $\frac{28}{63}$ reduced?**

    A) $\frac{7}{21}$

    B) $\frac{6}{9}$

    C) $\frac{4}{9}$

    D) $\frac{63}{28}$

14. **What is $\frac{3}{40}$ written as a decimal?**

    F) 0.75

    G) 7.50

    H) 750

    J) 0.075

15. **Which number is greater than 18.0454?**

    A) 18.0456

    B) 18.0453

    C) 18.0356

    D) 18.0321

16. **What is the missing number?**

    $\frac{16}{\square} = \frac{4}{5}$

    F) 25

    G) 64

    H) 10

    J) 20

17. **Written as a reduced fraction, 0.06 is—**

    A) $\frac{3}{50}$

    B) $\frac{6}{100}$

    C) $\frac{60}{100}$

    D) $\frac{6}{1000}$

18. **Which number tells how much of the figure below is shaded?**

    F) 0.25

    G) 0.33

    H) 0.65

    J) 0.80

STOP

Name _____   Date _____

MATH: MATH CONCEPTS
SAMPLE TEST

● **Directions:** Read each problem carefully. Select the correct answer.

Examples

A. **Which of these is another way to write the number in the box?**

| 32,000,000 + 6,000 + 400 + 2 |

- (A) 32,600,402
- (B) 32,642
- (C) 32,060,402
- (D) 32,006,402

B. **Which of these is greater than 6^3?**

- (F) 125
- (G) 200
- (H) 240
- (J) 205

Read and solve each problem carefully. Select the correct answer.

1. $\sqrt{121} =$
   - (A) 9
   - (B) 11
   - (C) 12
   - (D) 16

2. **What number is expressed by $(2 \times 10^3) + (6 \times 10^2) + (3 \times 10^1)$?**
   - (F) 2,630
   - (G) 263
   - (H) 2,063
   - (J) 26,063

3. $62,000 - 10,000 =$
   - (A) 25,000
   - (B) 50,200
   - (C) 72,000
   - (D) 52,000

4. **What is the prime factorization of 24?**
   - (F) 2 x 2 x 2 x 3
   - (G) 2 x 2 x 2 x 2 x 2
   - (H) 2 x 2 x 3
   - (J) 2 x 3 x 2

5. **Which of these numbers can you subtract from 28 to get a number less than ⁻4?**
   - (A) 30
   - (B) 36
   - (C) 18
   - (D) 28

6. **What are all of the factors of 24?**
   - (F) 2, 3, 6, 12
   - (G) 1, 3, 4, 12
   - (H) 1, 2, 3, 4, 12, 24
   - (J) 1, 2, 3, 4, 6, 8, 12, 24

GO ON

MATH: MATH CONCEPTS
SAMPLE TEST (cont.)

7. **What number completes this number sentence?**

   45 x 2 = _____ x 10

   (A) 9
   (B) 8
   (C) 7
   (D) 6

8. **Which of these is not a prime number?**

   (F) 19
   (G) 21
   (H) 23
   (J) 5

9. **In the problem below, each letter represents a certain number. What number does _P_ represent?**

   $$P + P + P + Q = 21$$
   $$Q + Q = 12$$

   (A) 4
   (B) 5
   (C) 6
   (D) 7

10. **Jeremy's average on his first 7 math quizzes was 86.429. What is the place value of the 9 in his average?**

    (F) tens
    (G) thousands
    (H) hundredths
    (J) thousandths

11. **Which of these number sentences is false?**

    (A) 8.65 > 8.56
    (B) 1.89 > 1.98
    (C) 5.65 > 5.56
    (D) 3.87 > 3.78

12. **150,000 + 50,000 =**

    (F) 100,000
    (G) 150,000
    (H) 200,000
    (J) 300,000

13. **What fraction is missing from the number pattern below?**

    $\frac{1}{10}$, $\frac{1}{5}$, $\frac{3}{10}$, $\frac{4}{10}$, _____ , $\frac{3}{5}$

    (A) $\frac{2}{3}$
    (B) $\frac{4}{5}$
    (C) $\frac{6}{10}$
    (D) $\frac{1}{2}$

GO ON

14. **What is the simplest name for $\frac{16}{24}$?**

- (F) $\frac{1}{3}$
- (G) $\frac{3}{4}$
- (H) $\frac{2}{3}$
- (J) $\frac{4}{5}$

15. **What is 78% expressed as a fraction?**

- (A) $\frac{1}{78}$
- (B) $\frac{78}{100}$
- (C) $\frac{78}{10}$
- (D) $\frac{78}{1000}$

16. **What is 16.06 written in words?**

- (F) sixteen and six hundredths
- (G) sixteen and six tenths
- (H) sixteen and zero hundredths
- (J) sixteen and six thousandths

17. **Written as a reduced fraction, 0.03 is—**

- (A) $\frac{30}{100}$
- (B) $\frac{3}{1000}$
- (C) $\frac{3}{1}$
- (D) $\frac{3}{100}$

18. **9,456 – 4,765 =**

- (F) 5,982
- (G) 4,236
- (H) 4,691
- (J) 5,245

19. **What is 0.76 rounded to the nearest tenth?**

- (A) 0.8
- (B) 0.7
- (C) 0.5
- (D) 0.760

20. **222.50 x 10.62 is closest to—**

- (F) 5,000
- (G) 3,500
- (H) 2,400
- (J) 4,000

21. **Which fraction shows what percentage of the shape below is shaded?**

- (A) $\frac{1}{2}$
- (B) $\frac{2}{3}$
- (C) $\frac{1}{3}$
- (D) $\frac{2}{5}$

STOP

MATH: COMPUTATION

● Lesson 4: Fractions, Addition and Subtraction

Directions: Solve each problem. Select the correct answer.

Examples

A. $\frac{2}{3} + \frac{1}{5} =$

Ⓐ $\frac{1}{2}$

Ⓑ $\frac{13}{19}$

Ⓒ $\frac{13}{15}$

Ⓓ $\frac{6}{14}$

B. $\frac{3}{4} - \frac{5}{8} =$

Ⓕ $\frac{1}{8}$

Ⓖ $\frac{3}{8}$

Ⓗ $\frac{1}{4}$

Ⓙ $\frac{1}{6}$

 Reduce your answers to simplest form.

● Practice

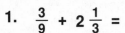

1. $\frac{3}{9} + 2\frac{1}{3} =$

Ⓐ $2\frac{2}{3}$

Ⓑ $2\frac{3}{5}$

Ⓒ $1\frac{1}{6}$

Ⓓ 2

2. $8\frac{2}{8} + 4\frac{1}{5} =$

Ⓕ $12\frac{1}{2}$

Ⓖ $10\frac{1}{3}$

Ⓗ $12\frac{9}{15}$

Ⓙ $12\frac{9}{20}$

3. $15\frac{3}{4} + 16\frac{1}{3} =$

Ⓐ $32\frac{1}{12}$

Ⓑ $32\frac{1}{3}$

Ⓒ $30\frac{1}{12}$

Ⓓ $28\frac{1}{6}$

4. $8 - 1\frac{5}{8} =$

Ⓕ $6\frac{1}{8}$

Ⓖ $6\frac{3}{8}$

Ⓗ $5\frac{1}{3}$

Ⓙ $7\frac{3}{5}$

5. $8\frac{3}{4} - 6\frac{2}{6} =$

Ⓐ $1\frac{5}{12}$

Ⓑ $2\frac{1}{12}$

Ⓒ $2\frac{5}{12}$

Ⓓ $1\frac{1}{2}$

6. $19\frac{2}{4} - 4\frac{2}{7} =$

Ⓕ $15\frac{1}{4}$

Ⓖ $14\frac{3}{4}$

Ⓗ $15\frac{2}{3}$

Ⓙ $15\frac{3}{14}$

STOP

MATH: COMPUTATION

● Lesson 5: Fractions, Multiplication and Division

Directions: Solve each problem. Select the correct answer.

Examples

A. $\frac{2}{3} \times \frac{1}{5} =$

(A) $\frac{4}{15}$

(B) $\frac{2}{15}$

(C) $\frac{1}{15}$

(D) 15

B. $\frac{2}{5} \div \frac{1}{10} =$

(F) 4

(G) 3

(H) 2

(J) 1

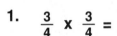 **Clue** Answers will be in simplest form.

● Practice

1. $\frac{3}{4} \times \frac{3}{4} =$

(A) $\frac{9}{16}$

(B) $\frac{3}{16}$

(C) $\frac{1}{13}$

(D) $\frac{1}{3}$

2. $2\frac{1}{3} \times 6 =$

(F) 13

(G) $\frac{1}{14}$

(H) 15

(J) 14

3. $1\frac{1}{4} \times 4\frac{1}{2} =$

(A) $5\frac{5}{8}$

(B) 5

(C) 5

(D) $6\frac{5}{8}$

4. $\frac{5}{6} \div \frac{3}{4} =$

(F) $1\frac{2}{9}$

(G) $\frac{1}{9}$

(H) $1\frac{1}{9}$

(J) $2\frac{1}{3}$

5. $4\frac{1}{2} \div 2\frac{3}{4} =$

(A) $1\frac{7}{11}$

(B) $1\frac{3}{11}$

(C) $1\frac{1}{11}$

(D) $2\frac{3}{4}$

6. $10 \div 3\frac{1}{3} =$

(F) $3\frac{1}{2}$

(G) 3

(H) $2\frac{2}{3}$

(J) $3\frac{1}{5}$

STOP

Name _____ Date _____

● **Lesson 6: Decimals, Addition and Subtraction**

Directions: Solve each problem. Select the correct answer.

Examples

A. 5.91 + 9.07 =   (A) 14.49
                     (B) 14.98
                     (C) 15.10
                     (D) 15.01

B. 28.9 – 19.7 =   (F) 8.7
                     (G) 9.2
                     (H) 9.5
                     (J) 9.6

 Clue Be certain to place the decimals in the correct place.

● **Practice**

1. 30.78 + 58.36 =

    (A) 98.01
    (B) 88.80
    (C) 89.00
    (D) 89.14

4. 37.86 – 31.49 =

    (F) 6.37
    (G) 6.00
    (H) 5.42
    (J) 5.96

2. 400.34 + 99.99 =

    (F) 500.33
    (G) 499.01
    (H) 499.10
    (J) 500.68

5. 100.01 – 84.56 =

    (A) 15.45
    (B) 15.22
    (C) 16.13
    (D) 17.02

3. 312.6 + 45.19 =

    (A) 356.62
    (B) 356.85
    (C) 357.79
    (D) 357.23

6. 308.02 – 177.25 =

    (F) 130.35
    (G) 129.10
    (H) 130.77
    (J) 230.67

STOP

Name _____ Date _____

MATH: COMPUTATION

● Lesson 7: Decimals, Multiplication and Division

Directions: Solve each problem. Select the correct answer, rounded to the nearest hundredth.

Examples

A. 5.91 x 0.07 =
- (A) 0.62
- (B) 0.41
- (C) 1.42
- (D) 0.09

B. 12.24 ÷ 0.02 =
- (F) 612.00
- (G) 621.00
- (H) 1.62
- (J) 16.20

 Clue Be certain to place the decimals in the correct places and round your answers to the nearest hundreth.

● Practice

1. 23.67 x 9.1 =
- (A) 215.40
- (B) 212.00
- (C) 315.41
- (D) 216.16

2. 707.47 x 8.87 =
- (F) 6,426.12
- (G) 5,275.00
- (H) 6,300.12
- (J) 6,275.26

3. 312.6 x 5.19 =
- (A) 1,622.39
- (B) 1,612.19
- (C) 1,515.29
- (D) 1,526.39

4. 5.55 ÷ 0.15 =
- (F) 3.70
- (G) 40.00
- (H) 32.00
- (J) 37.00

5. 23.7 ÷ 0.90 =
- (A) 28.20
- (B) 26.33
- (C) 24.70
- (D) 16.30

6. 15.12 ÷ 6 =
- (F) 3.50
- (G) 2.46
- (H) 2.52
- (J) 1.02

STOP

MATH: COMPUTATION

● Lesson 8: Percents, Converting to Decimals

Directions: Solve each problem. Change the percents to decimals. Select the correct answer.

Examples

A.	**60% =**	(A) 0.06	
		(B) 6	
		(C) 0.6	
		(D) 0.006	

B.	**4% =**	(F) 0.40	
		(G) 0.04	
		(H) 40.12	
		(J) 30	

 Clue Remember, percentages are always out of 100.

● Practice

1. **0.15% =**

(A) 0.15
(B) 15
(C) 0.0015
(D) 0.015

4. **5.67% =**

(F) 0.0567
(G) 0.567
(H) 56.7
(J) 567

2. **82.25% =**

(F) 82.25
(G) 42
(H) 8,225
(J) 0.8225

5. **.07% =**

(A) 0.07
(B) 7
(C) 0.007
(D) 0.0007

3. **13.75% =**

(A) 1.37
(B) 0.1375
(C) 1,375
(D) 137.5

6. $6\frac{2}{5}\% =$

(F) 6.4
(G) 0.625
(H) 0.064
(J) 0.0064

STOP

Name _____   Date _____

Lesson 9: Percents, Finding Percentages of a Number

Directions: Solve each problem. Change the percents to decimals to find the correct answers.

Examples

A.   10% of 2 =
- Ⓐ   2
- Ⓑ   0.02
- Ⓒ   0.002
- Ⓓ   0.2

B.   30% of 10 =
- Ⓕ   3
- Ⓖ   0.30
- Ⓗ   30
- Ⓙ   0.0003

 Clue Remember to change the percents to decimals to find the correct answers.

Practice

1.   6.32% of 1 =
- Ⓐ   0.632
- Ⓑ   0.0632
- Ⓒ   63.2
- Ⓓ   6.32

2.   10.45% of 20 =
- Ⓕ   2.19
- Ⓖ   2.09
- Ⓗ   0.0219
- Ⓙ   0.0209

3.   6% of $4\frac{1}{4}$ =
- Ⓐ   2.55
- Ⓑ   0.0255
- Ⓒ   0.255
- Ⓓ   20.55

4.   12.5% of 6 =
- Ⓕ   7.5
- Ⓖ   0.075
- Ⓗ   0.0075
- Ⓙ   0.75

5.   .03% of 20 =
- Ⓐ   0.006
- Ⓑ   6
- Ⓒ   0.6
- Ⓓ   0.06

6.   8% of 4.5 =
- Ⓕ   0.36
- Ⓖ   0.036
- Ⓗ   0.36
- Ⓙ   0.0036

 STOP

Name _____   Date _____

MATH: COMPUTATION

● Lesson 10: Problem Solving, Addition and Subtraction

Directions: Solve each problem. Select the correct answer.

Examples

A. Consider the numbers named by 0.328; 32.8; and 328. What is the sum of the two greatest numbers?

- (A) 328.3
- (B) 249.3
- (C) 388.8
- (D) 360.8

B. Kevin needs $1.43 to purchase a model car. He now has $0.75. How much more money does he need in order to buy the model car?

- (F) $0.68
- (G) $0.48
- (H) $2.18
- (J) $4.80

 Clue Read each problem carefully. Look for key words that help indicate whether you add or subtract.

● Practice

1. The odometer readings on three cars are 4,216.7; 382.4; and 53,318.6. According to the odometers, what is the total number of miles the cars were driven?

- (A) 57918.6
- (B) 57917.7
- (C) 64321.1
- (D) 56917.7

2. David made purchases at three stores. The amounts were $1.58, $3.97, and $0.97. What was the total amount of his purchases?

- (F) $6.52
- (G) $5.52
- (H) $6.53
- (J) $6.49

3. The population of Elmhurst is 43,526 and the population of Villa Park is 28,238. What is the combined population of the two towns?

- (A) 71,661
- (B) 71,762
- (C) 71,764
- (D) 70,763

4. Mrs. Harris drove 912 kilometers in May. She drove 1209 kilometers in June. How many more kilometers did she drive in June than in May?

- (F) 291
- (G) 397
- (H) 287
- (J) 297

STOP

MATH: COMPUTATION

● Lesson 11: Problem Solving, Multiplication and Division

Directions: Solve each problem. Select the correct answer.

Examples

A. There is 0.001 gram of iron in one egg. How much iron is there in 3 eggs?

- (A) 0.30
- (B) 0.03
- (C) 0.003
- (D) 30

B. A wire 15.3 meters long is to be separated into 9 pieces. Each piece is to be the same length. What will the length of each piece be in meters?

- (F) 2.7 meters
- (G) 1.7 meters
- (H) 17 meters
- (J) 0.17 meters

 Clue Read each problem carefully. Look for key words that help indicate whether you multiply or divide.

● Practice

1. Milo's car can be driven an average of 21.6 miles on each gallon of gasoline. How many miles can his car be driven on 9.8 gallons of gasoline?
   - (A) 112.68
   - (B) 201.68
   - (C) 211.68
   - (D) 21.68

2. A jet traveled at an average speed of 681 kilometers an hour. At that rate, how many kilometers did the jet go in 7.5 hours?
   - (F) 5,107.5
   - (G) 5,198.5
   - (H) 6,108.1
   - (J) 3,128.6

3. Six sheets of paper have a total thickness of 0.072 inches. Each sheet has the same thickness. What is the thickness, in inches, of each sheet?
   - (A) 0.012
   - (B) 0.12
   - (C) 12
   - (D) 12.12

4. The barometric pressure rose 1.44 in 3 hours. What was the average change per hour?
   - (F) 48
   - (G) 4.44
   - (H) 4.32
   - (J) 0.48

STOP

1-57768-977-1 — *Spectrum Test Practice 7*

Name _____ Date _____

● **Directions:** Solve each problem. Reduce fractions to lowest terms. Select the correct answer.

Examples

A. $\frac{4}{5} + \frac{1}{6} =$

- (A) $\frac{29}{30}$
- (B) $\frac{5}{11}$
- (C) $\frac{5}{24}$
- (D) $\frac{8}{9}$

B. $27.1 - 4.3 =$

- (F) 22.1
- (G) 22.8
- (H) 23
- (J) 23.7

---

1. $3\frac{1}{5} + 2\frac{3}{4} =$

- (A) $8\frac{2}{3}$
- (B) $4\frac{1}{4}$
- (C) $5\frac{19}{20}$
- (D) $6\frac{1}{4}$

2. $\frac{19}{20} + \frac{13}{20} =$

- (F) $\frac{1}{2}$
- (G) $\frac{3}{5}$
- (H) $1\frac{1}{2}$
- (J) $1\frac{3}{5}$

3. $45.36 \div 0.8 =$

- (A) 56.7
- (B) 5.67
- (C) 1.2
- (D) 5

4. $51.876 \div 0.055 =$

- (F) 819.1
- (G) 943.2
- (H) 600.2
- (J) 929.3

5. $33 \times 5.62 =$

- (A) 186.10
- (B) 190.32
- (C) 180.91
- (D) 185.46

6. $0.075 \times 100 =$

- (F) 7.5
- (G) 75
- (H) 7.005
- (J) 7.0005

GO ON

7. 0.005 + 3.79 + .4688 =

    (A) 4.2638
    (B) 4.8924
    (C) 3.668
    (D) 5.123

8. 1.2804 ÷ 0.33 =

    (F) 2.44
    (G) 3.66
    (H) 2.98
    (J) 3.88

9. 0.0041 + 0.9986 =

    (A) 1.0027
    (B) 1.2745
    (C) 2.7862
    (D) 1.3434

10. $\frac{20}{21} - \frac{2}{21} =$ (F) $\frac{3}{7}$

    (G) $\frac{6}{7}$

    (H) $\frac{1}{2}$

    (J) $\frac{22}{21}$

11. $\frac{4}{5} - \frac{1}{3} =$ (A) $\frac{7}{15}$

    (B) $\frac{3}{8}$

    (C) $\frac{9}{15}$

    (D) $\frac{3}{5}$

12. $3\frac{1}{5} + 7\frac{4}{5} + 2\frac{3}{5} =$

    (F) 13
    (G) $13\frac{1}{3}$
    (H) $13\frac{3}{5}$
    (J) $14\frac{1}{4}$

13. 60.35% =

    (A) 0.6351
    (B) 0.6513
    (C) 0.7526
    (D) 0.6035

14. 10% =

    (F) 10
    (G) 0.10
    (H) 1.1
    (J) 0.010

15. $1\frac{1}{4}$ % =

    (A) 1.50
    (B) 0.0125
    (C) 1.33
    (D) 2.25

16. .08% =

    (F) 0.08
    (G) 0.8
    (H) 0.0008
    (J) 8

GO ON

17. The thickness of a board is 0.037 meters. This is 0.014 meters less than what it is supposed to be. How thick is it supposed to be?

    (A) 51 m
    (B) 0.351 m
    (C) 0.62 m
    (D) 0.051 m

18. Two sheets of plastic have a combined thickness of 1.080 centimeters. One sheet is 0.675 centimeters thick. What is the thickness of the other sheet?

    (F) 0.405 cm
    (G) 0.12 cm
    (H) 40.5 cm
    (J) 0.302 cm

19. In 5 hours, 1.85 tons of ore were processed. The same amount was processed each hour. How many tons were processed each hour?

    (A) 0.27
    (B) 0.13
    (C) 0.25
    (D) 0.37

20. A gallon of water weighs about 8.34 pounds. Melissa used 21.5 gallons of water when she took a bath. What was the weight in pounds of the water she used?

    (F) 178.33
    (G) 179.31
    (H) 180.25
    (J) 179.60

21. Brigida earns $5.54 an hour. How much will she earn in 10 hours?

    (A) 55.32
    (B) 56.41
    (C) 55.40
    (D) 56.13

22. One package weighs 0.8 kilograms. Another weighs 0.6 kilograms. What is the combined weight in kilograms of these two packages?

    (F) 1.6
    (G) 2.1
    (H) 1.4
    (J) 0.9

23. Paul O'Neill had a batting average of .359 one season. Ken Griffey Jr.'s average was .323 that season. How much better was Paul O'Neill's average?

    (A) 0.036
    (B) 0.170
    (C) 0.029
    (D) 0.134

24. It costs $4.32 to mail a package that weighs 3 kilograms. What is the average cost per kilogram?

    (F) $1.46
    (G) $1.44
    (H) $1.32
    (J) $1.26

STOP

MATH: APPLICATIONS

● Lesson 12: Geometry

Directions: Read each problem carefully. Select the best answer.

Examples

A. What is the volume of a fish tank with a length of 3 meters, a height of 2 meters, and a width of 2 meters?

- Ⓐ 7 cubic meters
- Ⓑ 9 cubic meters
- Ⓒ 12 cubic meters
- Ⓓ 14 cubic meters

B. You know the measurements of two angles in a triangle. They are 39 degrees and 84 degrees. What is the measurement of the third angle?

- Ⓕ 180 degrees
- Ⓖ 123 degrees
- Ⓗ 57 degrees
- Ⓙ 40 degrees

 Clue If you are unsure of the answer, drawing on scratch paper may help you.

● Practice

1. Which statement about this triangle is true?

- Ⓐ Only one of the angles is an acute angle.
- Ⓑ Two of the angles are obtuse angles.
- Ⓒ There is one right and one acute angle.
- Ⓓ None of the angles are right angles.

2. A triangle is 27.2 centimeters high and 36 centimeters wide at its base. What is the area of the triangle?

- Ⓕ 979.2 square centimeters
- Ⓖ 489.6 square centimeters
- Ⓗ 73.2 square centimeters
- Ⓙ Not enough information

3. Which of the following is an obtuse angle?

Ⓐ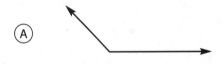

Ⓑ

Ⓒ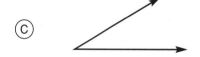

Ⓓ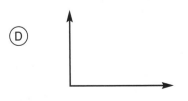

 GO ON

● **Lesson 12: Geometry (cont.)**

4. **What is the length *x* for the pair of similar triangles?**

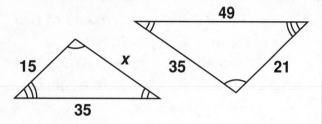

- (F) 35
- (G) 15
- (H) 25
- (J) 23

5. **What are the coordinates of point F?**

- (A) (6, 5)
- (B) (5, 6)
- (C) (4, 3)
- (D) (3, 4)

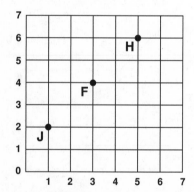

6. **What is the circumference of the circle below? Use 3.14 for π.**

- (F) 12.2 cm
- (G) 15.7 cm
- (H) 18.4 cm
- (J) 20.3 cm

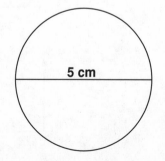

5 cm

7. **Which of the following shows how to bisect an angle?**

(A)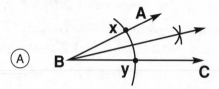

(B)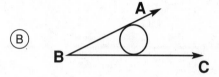

(C)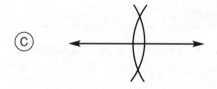

(D)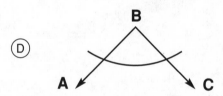

8. **Which of the following solid figures has *less* than 4 faces?**

- (F) a cube
- (G) a pyramid
- (H) a cone
- (J) a rectangular prism

GO ON

● **Lesson 12: Geometry (cont.)**

9. **Which of these shows a line segment?**

10. **Which of these formulas would help you find the length of side C of this right triangle?**

    Ⓕ $a + b = c$
    Ⓖ $a^2 + b = c$
    Ⓗ $a^2 + b^2 = c^2$
    Ⓙ $c^2 = a + b$

11. **What is the volume of this box ?**

    Ⓐ 120 cu. ft.
    Ⓑ 24 cu. ft.
    Ⓒ 110 cu. ft.
    Ⓓ 26 cu. ft.

    6 ft.   4 ft.   5 ft.

12. **The perimeter of this parallelogram is—**

    Ⓕ 88 inches
    Ⓖ 19 inches
    Ⓗ 38 inches
    Ⓙ 28 inches

    11 in.   8 in.

13. **Which set of lines below does not have the same length?**

    Ⓐ $\overline{BF}$ and $\overline{CD}$
    Ⓑ $\overline{BC}$ and $\overline{AC}$
    Ⓒ $\overline{FG}$ and $\overline{FH}$
    Ⓓ $\overline{FG}$ and $\overline{AC}$

    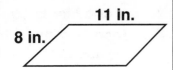

14. **Which of these angles is about 30°**

    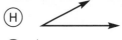

15. **Which of these is an octagon?**

    Ⓐ
    Ⓑ
    Ⓒ
    Ⓓ

16. **An obtuse angle is—**

    Ⓕ less than 90°
    Ⓖ greater than 90°
    Ⓗ the same as a right angle
    Ⓙ similar

17. **What shape will be formed if you fold the square on the right in half two times on the dashed lines?**

    Ⓐ a triangle
    Ⓑ a square
    Ⓒ a trapezoid
    Ⓓ a pentagon

18. **Look at the two squares below. What is the area of the shaded portion of the larger square?**

    Ⓕ 84 m²
    Ⓖ 40 m²
    Ⓗ 116 m²
    Ⓙ 30 m²

    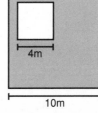
    4m   10m   STOP

Name _____ Date_____

● Lesson 13: Measurement

Directions: Read each problem carefully. Select the correct answer.

Examples

A. It takes 35 minutes to drive to the mall. You leave at 10:45. What time do you arrive?

- (A) 11:10
- (B) 11:20
- (C) 10:05
- (D) 11:30

B. In a foot, there are—

- (F) 3 yards
- (G) 12 centimeters
- (H) 12 inches
- (J) 11 inches

Clue Disregard information that you do not need to find the answer.

● Practice

1. Jamal is a football player. In one play, he ran the ball from the 63rd yard line to the 74th yard line. Then he ran the ball to the 92nd yard line. How far did Jamal run in all?

- (A) 29 yards
- (B) 32 yards
- (C) 35 yards
- (D) Not enough information

2. Kiki is running in a ten mile race. If she runs at her usual rate, how long will it take her to finish the race?

- (F) 1 hour and 15 minutes
- (G) 1 hour and 20 minutes
- (H) 1 hour and 30 minutes
- (J) Not enough information

3. What time does the clock show?

- (A) 9:50
- (B) 9:53
- (C) 10:49
- (D) 10:50

4. If one liter is equal to 1000 milliliters, then how many liters is 2500 milliliters?

- (F) 25 liters
- (G) 2.5 liters
- (H) 0.25 liters
- (J) 4 liters

GO ON

MATH: APPLICATIONS

● Lesson 13: Measurement (cont.)

5. Which of these represents the greatest mass?

    (A) 1.5 grams
    (B) 100 grams
    (C) 4.5 kilograms
    (D) 6 kilograms

6. About how big is a shoe box?

    (F) 6 inches by 14 inches by 8 inches
    (G) 2 inches by 20 inches by 1 inch
    (H) 6 inches by 25 inches by 8 inches
    (J) 3 inches by 14 inches by 6 inches

7. Which of these temperatures is the coolest?

    (A) ⁻6°
    (B) 0°
    (C) ⁻16°
    (D) ⁻5°

8. The perimeter of a rectangular room is 90 feet. If the length of the room is 35 feet, how wide is the room?

    (F) 8 feet
    (G) 10 feet
    (H) 20 feet
    (J) Not enough information

9. Tomas arrived at the museum at 9:15 and left $2\frac{1}{2}$ hours later. At what time did he leave the museum?

    (A) 11:15
    (B) 11:30
    (C) 11:45
    (D) 12:30

10. Quentin completed a 50-foot obstacle course in 30 seconds. At this rate how long would it take him to complete an 80-foot obstacle course?

    (F) 48 seconds
    (G) 60 seconds
    (H) 80 seconds
    (J) 110 seconds

11. Two quarts is equal to —

    (A) 8 pints
    (B) 1 gallon
    (C) 6 cups
    (D) 4 pints

12. Which of these statements is incorrect?

    (F) 0.5 liters is = 500 milliliters
    (G) 1 centimeter is = 0.5 meters
    (H) 1 kilometer is = 1000 meters
    (J) 1 milligram is = 0.001 grams

STOP

1-57768-977-1 — *Spectrum Test Practice 7*

Name _____ Date _____

MATH: APPLICATIONS

● Lesson 14: Problem Solving

Directions: Read each problem carefully. Select the correct answer.

Examples

A. What is the volume of a rectangular prism that is 3 ft. by 1.5 ft. by 2 ft.?

(A) 4 cubic feet
(B) 6.5 cubic feet
(C) 7.5 cubic feet
(D) 9 cubic feet

B. Two numbers have a sum of $8\frac{5}{12}$ and a product of $1\frac{3}{8}$. What are the two numbers?

(F) $\frac{2}{3}$ and $7\frac{1}{6}$
(G) $7\frac{3}{8}$ and $\frac{2}{3}$
(H) $8\frac{1}{4}$ and $\frac{1}{6}$
(J) $8\frac{1}{8}$ and $\frac{1}{12}$

 Clue Disregard information that you do not need to find the answer.

● Practice

1. Milton paid $19.96 for 4000 milliliters of grout. About how much did he pay per liter?

(A) $5.00
(B) $24.00
(C) $20.00
(D) $80.00

2. Which of these is the largest fraction?

(F) $\frac{2}{5}$
(G) $\frac{2}{7}$
(H) $\frac{2}{3}$
(J) $\frac{2}{9}$

3. A recipe for trail mix calls for 8 ounces of cereal, 3 ounces of dried fruit, and 5 ounces of nuts. About what fraction of the trail mix is cereal?

(A) $\frac{1}{4}$
(B) $\frac{1}{2}$
(C) $\frac{1}{3}$
(D) $\frac{2}{5}$

4. The students could buy pretzels at the game show. Miguel bought $3\frac{1}{2}$ pounds of pretzels at $1.20 per pound. How much did he pay for the pretzels?

(F) $0.42
(G) $1.42
(H) $4.20
(J) $42.00

GO ON

Name _____ Date _____

● Lesson 14: Problem Solving (cont.)

Use the table below to answer questions 5-7. Kim, Nicole, Ryan, and Rose were a team in which each child had to put together a five-piece puzzle. The team's total time was 85.2 seconds.

Name	Time
Kim	21.8 seconds
Nicole	18.9 seconds
Ryan	24.6 seconds
Rose	

5. What was Rose's time?

   Ⓐ 18.7 seconds
   Ⓑ 19.9 seconds
   Ⓒ 16.3 seconds
   Ⓓ 15.2 seconds

6. What was the team's average time?

   Ⓕ 21.30 seconds
   Ⓖ 22.16 seconds
   Ⓗ 18.09 seconds
   Ⓙ 22.26 seconds

7. How much longer did Ryan take to complete his puzzle than Kim?

   Ⓐ 1.8 seconds
   Ⓑ 3.2 seconds
   Ⓒ 2.4 seconds
   Ⓓ 2.8 seconds

8. Jeannie has twice as many compact discs as Stacey has. If t represents the number of compact discs Stacey has, what is the number of compact discs Jeannie has?

   Ⓕ $t + 2$
   Ⓖ $t - 2$
   Ⓗ $t \times 2$
   Ⓙ $t \div 2$

9. Two numbers have a product of 119,784 and a difference of 1,870. What are the two numbers?

   Ⓐ 2,791 and 921
   Ⓑ 3,864 and 31
   Ⓒ 1,932 and 62
   Ⓓ 1,496 and 394

10. Kelly's class wants to hold a carnival. They have saved $1,500 to host it. They will need $750 for equipment, $329 for food and beverages, and $192 to have posters and tickets made. How much money will they need to buy prizes for carnival attendants?

   Ⓕ $1,271.00
   Ⓖ $239.00
   Ⓗ $229.00
   Ⓙ Not enough information

11. A triangular shaped ship's sail is 54.6 meters high and 28.4 meters wide at its base. What is the area of the sail in meters?

   Ⓐ 689.5 meters
   Ⓑ 752.7 meters
   Ⓒ 862.6 meters
   Ⓓ 775.3 meters

12. How much change would you get from a $20 bill if you bought a pair of shorts for $9.98 and a tank top for $5.75?

   Ⓕ $15.73
   Ⓖ $4.27
   Ⓗ $3.76
   Ⓙ $5.25

GO ON

MATH: APPLICATIONS

● Lesson 14: Problem Solving (cont.)

13. George is doing a 10-mile walk for charity. Each of his 8 sponsors promises to pay him $1.50 for every mile that he walks. If he finishes the walk, how much money will he earn for charity?

   (A) $160.00
   (B) $80.00
   (C) $20.00
   (D) $120.00

14. A cube has 6 sides. 2 sides are red and 4 sides are blue. If you roll the cube, what are the odds that the red side will be facing up?

   (F) $\frac{1}{2}$
   (G) $\frac{1}{3}$
   (H) $\frac{2}{3}$
   (J) $\frac{1}{6}$

15. What is the total cost of a computer if the price is $900.00 and the tax is 5%?

   (A) $945.00
   (B) $905.00
   (C) $850.00
   (D) $950.00

16. Bob, an entomologist, has collected some ants, spiders, and centipedes. Ants have 6 legs, spiders have 8 legs, and centipedes have 100 legs. How many of each insect is there if there are 448 legs in all?

   (F) 32 ants, 7 spiders, 2 centipedes
   (G) 62 ants, 14 spiders, 1 centipede
   (H) 31 ants, 8 spiders, 2 centipedes
   (J) 34 ants, 6 spiders, 2 centipedes

17. A person needs about 2.5 quarts of water each day to survive. For how many days could a person survive on 40 quarts of water?

   (A) 100 days
   (B) 20 days
   (C) 16 days
   (D) 14 days

18. Nicole drinks 3.5 cups of milk each day. How many cups does she drink in one week?

   (F) 20.1
   (G) 23.5
   (H) 24.5
   (J) 18.5

STOP

Name _____ Date _____

● Lesson 15: Algebra

Directions: Read each problem carefully. Select the correct answer.

Examples

A. 5 more than 4 times *x* is 113. What is *x* ?

    (A) 25

    (B) 23

    (C) 28

    (D) 27

B. If 10 < *a* and *a* < *b*, what should replace the box in the expression 10 □ *b*?

    (F) >

    (G) <

    (H) =

    (J) –

 Clue Rework the problem if the solution you came up with does not match one of the answers.

● Practice

1. 34.6 ≥ ____

    (A) 35.2

    (B) 34.5

    (C) 36.4

    (D) 38.2

2. $|6 + 4| =$

    (F) ⁻10

    (G) ⁻6 + 4

    (H) |10|

    (J) 10 – (6 + 4)

3. 1,420 – 431 □ 2,168 – 520

    (A) =

    (B) %

    (C) >

    (D) <

4. The line is the graph for—

    (F) $x = y$

    (G) $x = y + 4$

    (H) $x = 8y$

    (J) $x = y + 2$

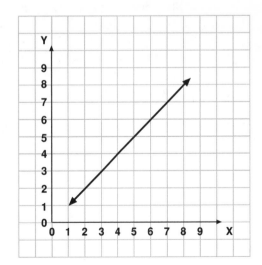

GO ON

MATH: APPLICATIONS

● **Lesson 15: Algebra (cont.)**

5. $9x - 6 = 21$
   $x =$
   - (A) 3
   - (B) 8
   - (C) 16
   - (D) -4

6. If $\frac{2}{3} = \frac{x}{12}$, then $x =$
   - (F) 9
   - (G) 4
   - (H) 6
   - (J) 8

7. Which of these shows how to find the number of hours (h) in 8 days?
   - (A) $24 \times 8 = h$
   - (B) $24 + 8 = h$
   - (C) $24 - 8 = h$
   - (D) $24 \div 8 = h$

8. $(6x + 1)^2 = 361$
   $x =$
   - (F) 2
   - (G) 3
   - (H) 4
   - (J) 5

9. What is $x \cdot x \cdot y \cdot y \cdot y \cdot y \cdot z$ written in exponential form?
   - (A) $x^2 y^3 z$
   - (B) $x^2 y^3 + z$
   - (C) $x y^2 z$
   - (D) $x^2 y^4 z$

10. Which equation means, "8 times a number is greater than 4 times the same number"?
    - (F) $(8 \times 4) < n$
    - (G) $8 + n < 4 + n$
    - (H) $4n < 8n$
    - (J) $4n > 8n$

11. If n is a whole number, which of these statements is true?
    - (A) If $n - 5 = 8$, then $10 \div n = 2$
    - (B) If $n + 5 = 8$, then $5 \div n = 5$
    - (C) If $n + 5 = 8$, then $9 \div n = 3$
    - (D) If $n + 8 = 5$, then $8 \div 3 = n$

12. If $x - 87 = 12$, then $x =$
    - (F) 102
    - (G) 99
    - (H) 75
    - (J) 53

STOP

Name _____   Date _____

MATH: APPLICATIONS
SAMPLE TEST

● **Directions:** Read each problem carefully. Select the correct answer.

Examples

A. Courtney gave the clerk a $20 bill. The amount of her purchases was $17.14. How much change should she receive?

- Ⓐ $2.69
- Ⓑ $2.86
- Ⓒ $3.86
- Ⓓ $1.29

B. The students went by van to the game show. Each van can hold 12 students. They completely filled 8 vans. How many students went to the game show?

- Ⓕ 20
- Ⓖ 96
- Ⓗ 100
- Ⓙ 120

---

1. How much of the figure is shaded?

- Ⓐ $\frac{1}{2}$
- Ⓑ $\frac{1}{4}$
- Ⓒ $\frac{1}{3}$
- Ⓓ $\frac{1}{8}$

2. If you wanted to compare the percentage of students who are going on a field trip to the percentage of students who are not going on a field trip, what would be the best graphic to use?

- Ⓕ a line graph
- Ⓖ a Venn diagram
- Ⓗ a pie chart
- Ⓙ not enough information

3. David's swimming pool is 42 feet long, 16 feet wide, and 8 feet deep. What is the volume of David's swimming pool?

- Ⓐ 66 cubic feet
- Ⓑ 5,376 cubic feet
- Ⓒ 15,376 cubic feet
- Ⓓ 28,502 cubic feet

4. 4,800 grams =

- Ⓕ 4.8 kilograms
- Ⓖ 48 kilograms
- Ⓗ 0.48 kilograms
- Ⓙ 0.48 milligrams

GO ON ➡

121

1-57768-977-1 — *Spectrum Test Practice 7*

Name _____   Date _____

Use the coordinate graph to answer questions 5 and 6.

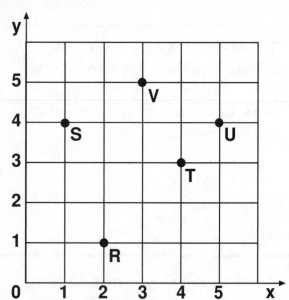

5. What point is at (3, 5)?

(A) R
(B) S
(C) V
(D) T

6. What are the coordinates of point S?

(F) (4,1)
(G) (2,1)
(H) (4,3)
(J) (1,4)

7. Which angle is a right angle?

(A)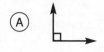

(B)

(C)

(D)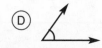

8. A round table has a diameter of 6 feet. What is the circumference of the table? Remember π = 3.14 and C = π x d.

(F) 18.00 feet
(G) 6.34 feet
(H) 12.00 feet
(J) 18.84 feet

9. What is the surface area of a cube if an edge is 8 centimeters long?

(A) 64 cm²
(B) 328 cm²
(C) 384 cm²
(D) 24 cm²

10. What is the average weight of three packages that weigh 120, 69, and 83 pounds?

(F) 90.7 pounds
(G) 85 pounds
(H) 98.3 pounds
(J) 99 pounds

11. You know the measurements of 2 angles in a triangle. They are 72 degrees and 42 degrees. What is the measurement of the third angle?

(A) 66 degrees
(B) 27 degrees
(C) 114 degrees
(D) 14 degrees

12. The distance around a mall is 1,800 yards. Which of these could be the length and width of the mall?

- (F) 600 yards and 100 yards
- (G) 500 yards and 400 yards
- (H) 200 yards and 500 yards
- (J) 400 yards and 200 yards

13. If $60y = ^-120$, then $y =$

- (A) 2
- (B) 60
- (C) $^-2$
- (D) $^-60$

14. Which equation means, "A number divided by itself is 1"?

- (F) $y \div y = 1$
- (G) $1 \div y = y$
- (H) $y^2 = 1$
- (J) $y \div 1 = y$

15. On a canoe trip with his family, Pete travels an average of 27 miles a day. If the final destination is 140 miles away, about how long will it take Pete to get there?

- (A) 2 days
- (B) 7 days
- (C) 5 days
- (D) 12 days

Use the line graph below to answer the questions 16–18.

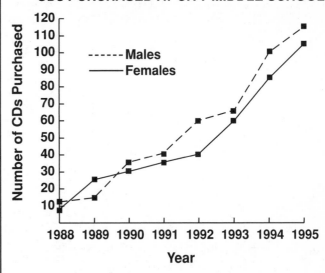

CDs PURCHASED AT CITY MIDDLE SCHOOL

16. How many CDs did the female students buy in 1990 and 1991?

- (F) about 100
- (G) about 65
- (H) about 43
- (J) about 35

17. In which year did the students buy 185 CDs?

- (A) 1988
- (B) 1990
- (C) 1994
- (D) 1992

18. How many CDs did the boys buy in 1990 and 1992?

- (F) 95
- (G) 60
- (H) 35
- (J) 80

STOP

ANSWER SHEET

STUDENT'S NAME		SCHOOL

LAST **FIRST** **MI**

TEACHER

FEMALE ◯   MALE ◯

(Name grid with letter bubbles A–Z in columns for LAST, FIRST, MI)

BIRTH DATE

MONTH	DAY	YEAR

JAN ◯
FEB ◯
MAR ◯
APR ◯
MAY ◯
JUN ◯
JUL ◯
AUG ◯
SEP ◯
OCT ◯
NOV ◯
DEC ◯

DAY: (0) (0) / (1) (1) / (2) (2) / (3) (3) / (4) / (5) / (6) / (7) / (8) / (9)

YEAR: (0) (1) (2) (3) (4) (5) (6) (7) (8) (9)   (5) (6) (7) (8) (9)

GRADE

⑥   ⑦   ⑧

Part 1: CONCEPTS

A Ⓐ Ⓑ Ⓒ Ⓓ
B Ⓕ Ⓖ Ⓗ Ⓙ
1 Ⓐ Ⓑ Ⓒ Ⓓ

2 Ⓕ Ⓖ Ⓗ Ⓙ
3 Ⓐ Ⓑ Ⓒ Ⓓ
4 Ⓕ Ⓖ Ⓗ Ⓙ

5 Ⓐ Ⓑ Ⓒ Ⓓ
6 Ⓕ Ⓖ Ⓗ Ⓙ
7 Ⓐ Ⓑ Ⓒ Ⓓ

8 Ⓕ Ⓖ Ⓗ Ⓙ
9 Ⓐ Ⓑ Ⓒ Ⓓ
10 Ⓕ Ⓖ Ⓗ Ⓙ

11 Ⓐ Ⓑ Ⓒ Ⓓ
12 Ⓕ Ⓖ Ⓗ Ⓙ
13 Ⓐ Ⓑ Ⓒ Ⓓ

14 Ⓕ Ⓖ Ⓗ Ⓙ

Part 2: COMPUTATION

A Ⓐ Ⓑ Ⓒ Ⓓ
B Ⓕ Ⓖ Ⓗ Ⓙ
1 Ⓐ Ⓑ Ⓒ Ⓓ
2 Ⓕ Ⓖ Ⓗ Ⓙ

3 Ⓐ Ⓑ Ⓒ Ⓓ
4 Ⓕ Ⓖ Ⓗ Ⓙ
5 Ⓐ Ⓑ Ⓒ Ⓓ
6 Ⓕ Ⓖ Ⓗ Ⓙ

7 Ⓐ Ⓑ Ⓒ Ⓓ
8 Ⓕ Ⓖ Ⓗ Ⓙ
9 Ⓐ Ⓑ Ⓒ Ⓓ
10 Ⓕ Ⓖ Ⓗ Ⓙ

11 Ⓐ Ⓑ Ⓒ Ⓓ
12 Ⓕ Ⓖ Ⓗ Ⓙ
13 Ⓐ Ⓑ Ⓒ Ⓓ
14 Ⓕ Ⓖ Ⓗ Ⓙ

15 Ⓐ Ⓑ Ⓒ Ⓓ
16 Ⓕ Ⓖ Ⓗ Ⓙ
17 Ⓐ Ⓑ Ⓒ Ⓓ
18 Ⓕ Ⓖ Ⓗ Ⓙ

Part 3: APPLICATIONS

A Ⓐ Ⓑ Ⓒ Ⓓ
B Ⓕ Ⓖ Ⓗ Ⓙ
1 Ⓐ Ⓑ Ⓒ Ⓓ

2 Ⓕ Ⓖ Ⓗ Ⓙ
3 Ⓐ Ⓑ Ⓒ Ⓓ
4 Ⓕ Ⓖ Ⓗ Ⓙ

5 Ⓐ Ⓑ Ⓒ Ⓓ
6 Ⓕ Ⓖ Ⓗ Ⓙ
7 Ⓐ Ⓑ Ⓒ Ⓓ

8 Ⓕ Ⓖ Ⓗ Ⓙ
9 Ⓐ Ⓑ Ⓒ Ⓓ
10 Ⓕ Ⓖ Ⓗ Ⓙ

11 Ⓐ Ⓑ Ⓒ Ⓓ
12 Ⓕ Ⓖ Ⓗ Ⓙ
13 Ⓐ Ⓑ Ⓒ Ⓓ

14 Ⓕ Ⓖ Ⓗ Ⓙ

1-57768-977-1 — Spectrum Test Practice 7

Name _____ Date _____

● **Part 1: Concepts**

Directions: Read each problem carefully. Select the correct answer.

Examples

A. What is another way to write 40,000,000 + 6,000,000 + 30,000 + 200 + 2?

- (A) 46,322
- (B) 4,603,020
- (C) 46,030,202
- (D) 40,632,200

B. Which of these decimals is less than 2.775 and greater than 1.865?

- (F) 0.612
- (G) 2.235
- (H) 1.635
- (J) 0.023

---

1. Which of the following is another name for $\frac{19}{5}$?

- (A) $3\frac{4}{5}$
- (B) $2\frac{4}{5}$
- (C) $3\frac{5}{19}$
- (D) $3\frac{19}{5}$

2. Which of these is a factor of 16, 32, and 64?

- (F) 3
- (G) 8
- (H) 5
- (J) 6

3. Which of these number sentences could be used to find the missing number in the pattern below?

1, 4, 7, 10, 13, 16, _____, 22

- (A) $19 - 6 = 13$
- (B) $16 - 3 = 13$
- (C) $16 + 3 = 19$
- (D) $21 - 4 = 18$

4. Which of these is the best estimate of the percentage of the circle that is not shaded?

- (F) 50%
- (G) 25%
- (H) 33%
- (J) 75%

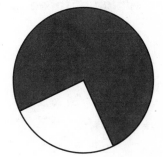

5. $4.2 \times 10^3 =$

- (A) 42
- (B) 42,000
- (C) 4,200
- (D) 420

6. $6^3 - 24 =$

- (F) 192
- (G) 292
- (H) 0
- (J) 12

GO ON →

MATH PRACTICE TEST
Part 1: Concepts (cont.)

7. Which of these is <u>not</u> another way to write $\frac{18}{24}$?

   (A) 0.25

   (B) 75%

   (C) $\frac{3}{4}$

   (D) 0.75

8. What is the prime factorization of 32?

   (F) 2 x 2 x 2 x 2

   (G) 2 x 2 x 2 x 2 x 2

   (H) 2 x 2 x 2 x 3

   (J) 2 x 2 x 2 x 2 x 2 x 2

9. Which of these is the best estimate of

   $25.15 \times 5\frac{6}{7}$

   (A) 25 x 6

   (B) 24 x 5

   (C) 26 x 7

   (D) 25 x 4

10. Which of these is another way to write 0.12?

    (F) 1.2%

    (G) 0.012

    (H) 120%

    (J) 12%

11. What should replace the box in the equation

    21,014 = 20,000 + □ + 10 + 4

    (A) 0

    (B) 10

    (C) 100

    (D) 1,000

12. Which of these is two ten-thousandths?

    (F) 0.0002

    (G) 0.0020

    (H) 2.0000

    (J) 0.2000

13. What does the *n* in the equation below stand for?

    (*n* + 6) x 8 = (8 x 2) + (8 x 6)

    (A) 3

    (B) 2

    (C) 4

    (D) 6

14. $\sqrt{256} =$

    (F) 18

    (G) 12

    (H) 14

    (J) 16

STOP

Name _____ Date_____

● **Part 2: Computation**

   Directions: Read each problem carefully. Select the correct answer.

Examples

A.	46.87 + 59.06 =	(A)	104.96		B.	83 − 0.59 =	(F)	82.41
		(B)	105.93				(G)	81.98
		(C)	103.03				(H)	82.64
		(D)	113.26				(J)	83.02

1.	0.863 + 0.136 =	(A)	0.899		5.	24.6929 x 10 =	(A)	24.6
		(B)	0.789				(B)	2.46
		(C)	0.999				(C)	246.929
		(D)	0.629				(D)	246.299

2.	21.2 x 63 =	(F)	1,233.1		6.	72.05 + 0.008 =	(F)	71.063
		(G)	2,611.4				(G)	72.058
		(H)	1,235.2				(H)	72.896
		(J)	1,335.6				(J)	70.113

3.	25 x 0.25 =	(A)	6.25		7.	34.37 ÷ 5 =	(A)	6.874
		(B)	6				(B)	6.213
		(C)	5.50				(C)	5.999
		(D)	6.75				(D)	8.245

4.	3.6 ÷ 12 =	(F)	3		8.	0.056 x 100 =	(F)	5
		(G)	0.6				(G)	5.2
		(H)	0.2				(H)	4.8
		(J)	0.3				(J)	5.6

GO ON

MATH PRACTICE TEST
Part 2: Computation (cont.)

9.   4 x 12 ÷ 6 =

(A) 8

(B) 10

(C) 6

(D) 4

10. $4 \frac{4}{5} + 3 \frac{2}{5}$ =

(F) $7 \frac{1}{6}$

(G) $8 \frac{2}{5}$

(H) $8 \frac{1}{5}$

(J) $6 \frac{2}{3}$

11. $1 \frac{3}{4} + 2 \frac{3}{4} + 1 \frac{1}{4}$ =

(A) $5 \frac{1}{2}$

(B) $5 \frac{3}{4}$

(C) $4 \frac{3}{4}$

(D) $3 \frac{1}{3}$

12. 10,469 + 9,400 + 32 =

(F) 19,000

(G) 18,469

(H) 19,901

(J) 19,981

13. 0.20 x 5 =

(A) 1

(B) 2

(C) 4

(D) 3

14. $20 \frac{3}{4} - 3 \frac{1}{4}$ =

(F) $17 \frac{1}{2}$

(G) $16 \frac{3}{4}$

(H) $15 \frac{1}{2}$

(J) $17 \frac{3}{4}$

15. 14% of 30 =

(A) 4.4

(B) 2.6

(C) 4.8

(D) 4.2

16. 85% of 110 =

(F) 93.25

(G) 92.10

(H) 94.6

(J) 93.5

17. 0.2 x 95 =

(A) 19

(B) 21

(C) 17

(D) 12

18. 4.5% of 17 =

(F) 0.832

(G) 0.765

(H) 0.236

(J) 0.625

STOP

Name _____   Date _____

● **Part 3: Applications**

Directions: Read each problem carefully. Select the correct answer.

Examples

A. The distance around a swimming pool is 90 feet. Which of these could be the length and width of the pool?

(A) 20 feet and 15 feet

(B) 15 feet and 40 feet

(C) 30 feet and 15 feet

(D) 25 feet and 25 feet

B. What is the surface area of a cube if an edge is 4 centimeters long?

(F) 12 cm²

(G) 96 cm²

(H) 100 cm²

(J) 36 cm²

---

1. An irregularly shaped pentagon has a perimeter of 764 meters. The pentagon has sides that are 129 meters, 365 meters, 24 meters, and 100 meters long. What is the length of the fifth side?

(A) 146 meters

(B) 177 meters

(C) 1,389 meters

(D) 22 meters

2. The perimeter of the room in which the party will take place is 70 feet. The width is 15 feet. What is the length?

(F) 40 feet

(G) 30 feet

(H) 20 feet

(J) 10 feet

3. What is the probability that this spinner will stop on 2?

(A) $\frac{1}{4}$

(B) $\frac{1}{3}$

(C) $\frac{1}{2}$

(D) 1

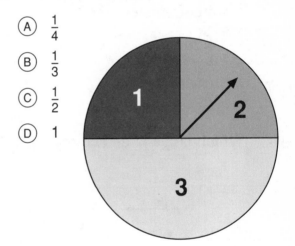

4. An angle of 86° is—

(F) symmetric

(G) right

(H) obtuse

(J) acute

GO ON

5. If $10y = 80$, then $y =$
    - (A) 4
    - (B) 2
    - (C) 6
    - (D) 8

6. If x is a positive whole number, and
    $\frac{20}{x} = \frac{x}{5}$, then $x =$
    - (F) 30
    - (G) 25
    - (H) 125
    - (J) 10

7. Which of these is the warmest temperature?
    - (A) 16° F
    - (B) 10° F
    - (C) 0° F
    - (D) ⁻8° F

8. Which angle is an acute angle?
    - (F)
    - (G)
    - (H)
    - (J)

9. Which equation means, "A number multiplied by itself is 64"?
    - (A) $y^2 = 64$
    - (B) $y + y = 64$
    - (C) $y \times 64 = y$
    - (D) $y \times 0 = 64$

10. A construction crew is building a house that is 30 feet by 60 feet. They have finished 900 square feet of the project. What percentage of the house is unfinished?
    - (F) 50%
    - (G) 25%
    - (H) 60%
    - (J) 75%

11. If $x = 14$, then $2 + 6x =$
    - (A) 86
    - (B) 81
    - (C) 75
    - (D) 89

12. 1,400 grams =
    - (F) 14 kilograms
    - (G) 14,000 kilograms
    - (H) 1.4 kilograms
    - (J) 0.14 kilograms

13. What is the perimeter of this parallelogram?
    - (A) 24 inches
    - (B) 16 inches
    - (C) 28 inches
    - (D) 32 inches

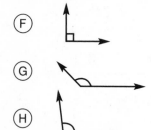

7 inches
9 inches

14. If a cube has 3 red sides and 3 blue sides and you roll the cube 10 times, how many times will it land with the red facing up?
    - (F) 5
    - (G) 10
    - (H) 7
    - (J) 3

STOP

SCIENCE

● Lesson 1: General Knowledge

Directions: Read each question carefully. Select the best answer for each question.

Examples

A. A graduated cylinder is used to measure the—	B. The three phases of matter are solid, gas, and—
Ⓐ volume of a liquid.	Ⓕ suspension.
Ⓑ weight of a liquid.	Ⓖ liquid.
Ⓒ mass of a liquid.	Ⓗ precipitation.
Ⓓ weight of a solid.	Ⓙ gel.

 Clue If you are unsure of the answer, skip the question and come back to it later.

● Practice

1. The meter is the basic measure of—

   Ⓐ mass.

   Ⓑ weight.

   Ⓒ length.

   Ⓓ volume.

2. The boiling temperature of water in degrees Celsius is—

   Ⓕ 32°C

   Ⓖ 0°C

   Ⓗ 100°C

   Ⓙ 212°C

3. Which of the following steps of the scientific method would follow conducting an experiment?

   Ⓐ researching the problem

   Ⓑ making a hypothesis

   Ⓒ writing a conclusion

   Ⓓ collecting data

4. The gram is the basic unit of—

   Ⓕ mass.

   Ⓖ volume.

   Ⓗ length.

   Ⓙ weight.

GO ON

Name _____ Date _____

● Lesson 1: General Knowledge (cont.)

5. The liter is the basic unit of—

   Ⓐ volume.

   Ⓑ length.

   Ⓒ weight.

   Ⓓ mass.

6. Which of these measurements would vary if taken on the earth and then on the moon?

   Ⓕ mass only

   Ⓖ weight only

   Ⓗ mass and weight

   Ⓙ length and width

7. One thousand milligrams is equal to _____ gram(s).

   Ⓐ 10

   Ⓑ 100

   Ⓒ 100

   Ⓓ 1

8. Which of the following is needed to calculate the density of a substance?

   Ⓕ weight and volume

   Ⓖ volume and speed

   Ⓗ speed and mass

   Ⓙ mass and volume

9. _____ is the energy of position.

   Ⓐ Kinetic

   Ⓑ Potential

   Ⓒ Solar

   Ⓓ Heat

10. _____ is the energy of motion.

    Ⓕ Kinetic

    Ⓖ Potential

    Ⓗ Solar

    Ⓙ Heat

GO ON

SCIENCE

● **Lesson 1: General Knowledge (cont.)**

11. **Velocity is a measurement of—**
    - (A) the amount of mass of an object.
    - (B) the energy of an object.
    - (C) the attractive force of an object.
    - (D) the speed of an object.

12. **Gravity is a measurement of—**
    - (F) the distance between two objects.
    - (G) the energy between two objects.
    - (H) the attractive force of an object.
    - (J) the acceleration of an object.

13. **Scissors are an example of a(n)—**
    - (A) inclined plane
    - (B) pulley
    - (C) wheel and axle
    - (D) lever

14. **A twist-off bottle cap is an example of a(n)—**
    - (F) pulley.
    - (G) inclined plane.
    - (H) screw.
    - (J) lever.

15. **_____ is the chemical formula for water.**
    - (A) H_2
    - (B) NH_3
    - (C) OH
    - (D) H_2O

16. **_____ is the chemical formula for carbon dioxide.**
    - (F) CO_2
    - (G) CH_3
    - (H) CO
    - (J) CH_4

STOP

SCIENCE

● Lesson 2: Reading and Understanding

Directions: Read the passages and select the best answer for each question.

Example

The Earth rotates around an imaginary axis through the North and South Poles. You can also consider the Earth as revolving around another imaginary axis through the center of the orbit and perpendicular to the plane of the orbit.

A. **How many axes are described in the passage?**
- (A) two
- (B) three
- (C) one
- (D) four

 If you are unsure of the answer, skim the passage again.

● Practice

Sir Isaac Newton

Sir Isaac Newton, born in 1642, was an English scientist, astronomer, and mathematician. Newton is sometimes described as "one of the greatest names in the history of human thought" because of his great contributions to mathematics, physics, and astronomy.

Newton discovered how the universe is held together through his theory of gravitation. He discovered the secrets of light and color, and he invented a new kind of mathematics, *calculus*. Newton made these three discoveries within 18 months from 1665 to 1667.

1. **To which of the following did Isaac Newton not contribute?**
   - (A) mathematics
   - (B) physics
   - (C) astronomy
   - (D) biology

2. **Newton discovered the secrets of—**
   - (F) light and dark
   - (G) light and color
   - (H) night and day
   - (J) color and hue

3. **Newton was born in—**
   - (A) 1842
   - (B) 1642
   - (C) 1624
   - (D) 1726

4. **Write a few sentences that tell what you know about gravity.**

   _____

   _____

   _____

   _____

   _____

GO ON

SCIENCE

● Lesson 2: Reading and Understanding (cont.)

The brain has three main divisions: the cerebrum, the cerebellum, and the brain stem. Each part consists chiefly of nerve cells, called *neurons*, and supporting cells, called *gila*.

5. **The three divisions of the brain consist mainly of—**

    (A) atoms.

    (B) cerebellums.

    (C) stems and gila.

    (D) neurons and gila.

Refer back to the passage if you need to.

Brain Cells

The human brain has from 10 billion to 100 billion neurons. All of these neurons are present within a few months after birth. After a person reaches about 20 years of age, some neurons die or disappear each day. In general, neurons that die are not replaced during a person's lifetime. Over a lifetime, however, this loss equals less than 10 percent of all the neurons.

The brain's billions of neurons connect with one another in complex networks. All physical and mental functioning depends on the establishment and maintenance of neuron networks. A person's habits and skills — such as nail biting or playing a musical instrument — become embedded within the brain in frequently activated neuron networks. When a person stops performing an activity, the neural networks for the activity fall into disuse and eventually may disappear.

6. **The human brain has more than—**

    (A) 100 billion neurons.

    (B) 10 billion neurons.

    (C) 10 billion networks.

    (D) 10 trillion neurons.

7. **All neurons are present a few months after—**

    (F) age 69.

    (G) death.

    (H) birth.

    (J) adolescence.

8. **The neurons connect with one another in complex—**

    (A) instruments.

    (B) systems.

    (C) carbohydrates.

    (D) networks.

9. **Describe another habit or skill that would be embedded within the brain. Tell why the neural networks for this habit or skill would or would not fall away if the activity was stopped.**

_____

_____

_____

_____

_____

_____

_____

GO ON

SCIENCE

● Lesson 2: Reading and Understanding (cont.)

Weather forecasters study clouds carefully because certain types often appear before storms. In many cases, a warm front or low pressure system may be identified by these clouds.

10. **A warm front can be identified by—**
- (A) a certain type of cloud.
- (B) a cold front.
- (C) a high pressure system.
- (D) a heavy snow storm.

Read the passage and try to remember the details.

How Clouds Form

Clouds form from water that has evaporated from lakes, oceans, and rivers, or from moist soil and plants. This evaporated water, called *water vapor*, expands and cools as it rises into the air. Air can hold only a certain amount of water vapor at any given temperature. Warm air can hold more water vapor than cool air can. When the temperature drops, some of the water vapor begins to *condense* (change to a liquid) into tiny water droplets.

For water vapor to condense, particles so small they can be seen only through a microscope must be present. These particles, called condensation nuclei, become the centers of the droplets. Many *condensation nuclei* are tiny salt particles or small particles present in smoke. Most droplets measure from 1/2,500 to 1/250 inch (0.01 to 0.1 millimeter) in diameter.

11. **Evaporated water is called—**
- (A) condensation.
- (B) particles.
- (C) vapor.
- (D) droplets.

12. **Warm air can hold more water vapor than—**
- (F) cool air.
- (G) a rain cloud.
- (H) a particle.
- (J) a condensation nuclei.

13. **To condense means to change to a—**
- (A) gas.
- (B) solid.
- (C) vapor.
- (D) liquid.

14. **Many condensation nuclei are—**
- (F) hail.
- (G) salt particles.
- (H) snow flurries.
- (J) larger than 1/25 of an inch diameter.

STOP

Name _____   Date_____

SCIENCE

SAMPLE TEST

● **Directions:** Read each question carefully. Select the best answer.

Examples

A. **Which of the following minerals is the hardest?**
- Ⓐ talc
- Ⓑ quartz
- Ⓒ diamond
- Ⓓ gypsum

B. **The three body sections of an insect are the—**
- Ⓕ head, abdomen, and legs.
- Ⓖ abdomen, legs, and thorax.
- Ⓗ head, thorax, and abdomen.
- Ⓙ head, legs, and thorax.

1. **Complete metamorphosis differs from incomplete metamorphosis in that—**
- Ⓐ The larva form does not resemble the adult form during complete metamorphosis.
- Ⓑ A nymph is present during complete metamorphosis.
- Ⓒ Eggs are not present during complete metamorphosis.
- Ⓓ The adult form resembles the larva form during complete metamorphosis.

2. **During photosynthesis, plants use the sun's energy, water, and carbon dioxide to make—**
- Ⓕ oxygen only.
- Ⓖ sugar only.
- Ⓗ sugar and carbon.
- Ⓙ sugar and oxygen.

3. **One thousand grams is equal to ____ kilogram(s).**
- Ⓐ 10
- Ⓑ 100
- Ⓒ 1000
- Ⓓ 1

4. **One thousand milliliters is equal to ____ liter(s).**
- Ⓕ 1
- Ⓖ 10
- Ⓗ 100
- Ⓙ 1000

5. The tides are created mostly by the—
   - (A) sun.
   - (B) moon.
   - (C) stars.
   - (D) asteroid belt.

6. Which class of vertebrate is characterized as being warm-blooded, hatched, and breathes using lungs?
   - (F) mammals
   - (G) birds
   - (H) fish
   - (J) reptiles

7. The part of the plant that absorbs water and nutrients from the soil is the—
   - (A) flower.
   - (B) leaf.
   - (C) root.
   - (D) stem.

8. What does a barometer measure?
   - (F) water depth
   - (G) atmospheric moisture
   - (H) atmospheric pressure
   - (J) water temperature

9. What do our bones help with?
   - (A) protection
   - (B) support
   - (C) production of blood cells
   - (D) all of the above

10. A crack in the earth's bedrock is know as a—
    - (F) fault.
    - (G) continent.
    - (H) fracture.
    - (J) volcano.

11. Explain why making a hypothesis before conducting an experiment is an important part of the scientific method.

    _____

    _____

    _____

    _____

    _____

    _____

    _____

STOP

STUDENT'S NAME

| LAST | FIRST | MI |

(Bubble grid A–Z for each letter column)

SCHOOL

TEACHER

FEMALE ◯   MALE ◯

BIRTH DATE

MONTH	DAY	YEAR

JAN ◯
FEB ◯
MAR ◯
APR ◯
MAY ◯
JUN ◯
JUL ◯
AUG ◯
SEP ◯
OCT ◯
NOV ◯
DEC ◯

DAY: (0) (0), (1) (1), (2) (2), (3) (3), (4), (5), (6), (7), (8), (9)

YEAR: (0), (1), (2), (3), (4), (5) (5), (6) (6), (7) (7), (8) (8), (9) (9)

GRADE

(6)   (7)   (8)

SCIENCE

A	Ⓐ Ⓑ Ⓒ Ⓓ	4	Ⓕ Ⓖ Ⓗ Ⓙ	9	Ⓐ Ⓑ Ⓒ Ⓓ
B	Ⓕ Ⓖ Ⓗ Ⓙ	5	Ⓐ Ⓑ Ⓒ Ⓓ	10	Ⓕ Ⓖ Ⓗ Ⓙ
1	Ⓐ Ⓑ Ⓒ Ⓓ	6	Ⓕ Ⓖ Ⓗ Ⓙ		
2	Ⓕ Ⓖ Ⓗ Ⓙ	7	Ⓐ Ⓑ Ⓒ Ⓓ		
3	Ⓐ Ⓑ Ⓒ Ⓓ	8	Ⓕ Ⓖ Ⓗ Ⓙ		

Name _____   Date_____

SCIENCE PRACTICE TEST

● **Directions:** Read each question carefully. Select the correct answer.

Examples

A. **Which of the following tools would be used to study cells?**

   Ⓐ telescope
   Ⓑ microscope
   Ⓒ binoculars
   Ⓓ thermometer

B. **The photosynthetic layer of leaves is the—**

   Ⓕ vein.
   Ⓖ palisade layer.
   Ⓗ epidermis.
   Ⓙ spongy layer.

1. **The mass number of an atom equals the number of _____ in the nucleus of the atom.**

   Ⓐ protons and electrons

   Ⓑ electrons and neutrons

   Ⓒ protons and neutrons

   Ⓓ electrons and protons

2. **Which planet has a large storm known as the "Great Red Spot"?**

   Ⓕ Saturn

   Ⓖ Earth

   Ⓗ Jupiter

   Ⓙ Mars

3. **A solar eclipse occurs when—**

   Ⓐ the moon is directly between the earth and the sun.

   Ⓑ the sun is directly between the earth and the moon.

   Ⓒ the earth is directly between the sun and the moon.

   Ⓓ the earth, sun, and moon are not directly in a line.

4. **The four planets closest to the sun are Mercury, Venus, Earth, and—**

   Ⓕ Jupiter.

   Ⓖ Mars.

   Ⓗ Uranus.

   Ⓙ Neptune.

SCIENCE PRACTICE TEST
(cont.)

5. **Groups of stars that appear to outline a picture are known as—**

   (A) asteroids.

   (B) dirty snowballs.

   (C) galaxies.

   (D) constellations.

6. **Rock that is formed by the hardening of sediments is called—**

   (F) metamorphic rock.

   (G) sedimentary rock.

   (H) igneous rock.

   (J) magma.

7. **Which of the following is characteristic of the human circulatory system?**

   (A) lungs, 2 atriums, 2 ventricles

   (B) lungs, 2 atriums, ventricle

   (C) gills, ventricle, atrium

   (D) breath though skin, no ventricle, no atrium

8. **The five kingdom categories are fungi, monerans, plants, animals, and—**

   (F) bacteria.

   (G) viruses.

   (H) amoebas.

   (J) protists.

9. **Which of the following is not an invertebrate?**

   (A) clam

   (B) worm

   (C) starfish

   (D) frog

10. **A light year is—**

    (F) a measure of time.

    (G) the measure of the speed of light.

    (H) the distance light travels in one year.

    (J) none of the above.

11. **Explain why sound travels more quickly through warm air than in cold air.**

    _____

    _____

    _____

    _____

    _____

    _____

    _____

STOP

Name _____   Date_____

SOCIAL STUDIES

● Lesson 1: General Knowledge

Directions: Read each question carefully. Select the best answer.

Examples

A. The quote "give me your tired, your poor, your hungry . . . " is part of which American symbol?

- (A) Great Seal of the United States
- (B) Statue of Liberty
- (C) National Anthem
- (D) Liberty Bell

B. Which of the following is not a purpose of the government according to the Preamble to the Constitution?

- (F) to form a more perfect union
- (G) to establish justice
- (H) to provide education for all
- (J) to provide for common defense

 Clue If you are unsure of the answer, skip the question and come back to it later.

● Practice

1. Who was elected president of the Constitutional Convention?

- (A) James Madison
- (B) Thomas Jefferson
- (C) George Washington
- (D) Benjamin Franklin

2. A _____ is government by the people.

- (F) republic
- (G) democracy
- (H) federalism
- (J) checks and balances

3. A division of governmental powers in which each branch has some control and influence over the others' power is called—

- (A) checks and balances.
- (B) separation of power.
- (C) democracy.
- (D) federalism.

4. What is a division of governmental powers among the legislative, executive, and judicial branches called?

- (F) constitutional government
- (G) New Jersey Plan
- (H) federalism
- (J) separation of power

GO ON

SOCIAL STUDIES

● Lesson 1: General Knowledge (cont.)

5. **The Nineteenth Amendment did what?**

   (A) kept people from voting

   (B) repealed the Eighteenth Amendment

   (C) did away with slavery

   (D) gave women the right to vote

6. **To be accepted as part of the Constitution, a proposed amendment must be ratified by what fraction of the states?**

   (F) one third

   (G) three fourths

   (H) two thirds

   (J) over fifty percent

7. **Which of the following is not one of the three branches of government?**

   (A) executive

   (B) judicial

   (C) defense

   (D) legislative

8. **Another name for <u>legislature</u> is—**

   (F) Congress.

   (G) presidential.

   (H) federal.

   (J) executive.

9. **The U.S. Constitution created a federal government that divided the powers between—**

   (A) national and state governments.

   (B) national and local governments.

   (C) state and local governments.

   (D) national and foreign governments.

10. **Federal, state, and local governments of the United States have—**

    (F) no limits on their power.

    (G) one judge.

    (H) legal limits on their power.

    (J) use of intimidation.

GO ON

SOCIAL STUDIES

● **Lesson 1: General Knowledge (cont.)**

11. **Who heads the executive branch of the United States?**

    Ⓐ president

    Ⓑ vice-president

    Ⓒ secretary of state

    Ⓓ treasurer

12. **How did the framers of the Constitution try to avoid misuse of presidential power?**

    Ⓕ by passing a law

    Ⓖ by giving women the right to vote

    Ⓗ by creating three branches of power

    Ⓙ by preserving the constitution

13. **The *Reformation* was not a—**

    Ⓐ religious revolt.

    Ⓑ peaceful time.

    Ⓒ time of fear.

    Ⓓ time of change.

14. **Which one of the following is not in or near the Fertile Crescent, a region of ancient Mesopotamia?**

    Ⓕ Tigris River

    Ⓖ Euphrates River

    Ⓗ Gulf of Mexico

    Ⓙ Mediterranean Sea

15. **The term *renaissance* means—**

    Ⓐ painting.

    Ⓑ intellectual.

    Ⓒ music.

    Ⓓ rebirth.

16. **Which of the following is not one of the Seven Wonders of the Ancient World?**

    Ⓕ Colossus of Rhodes

    Ⓖ Pyramids of Egypt at Giza

    Ⓗ Great Wall of China

    Ⓙ Lighthouse of Alexandria

17. **The caste system in India places people in different ranks of society. Write a paragraph comparing this system to what you are accustomed to in the United States.**

    _____

    _____

    _____

    _____

    _____

    _____

    _____

STOP

SOCIAL STUDIES

● Lesson 2: Reading and Understanding

Directions: Read the passages and select the best answer for each question.

Example

The U.S. Constitution sets forth how the American people will pay for government. It is through taxation. For a long time, the only way Congress got money to pay debts and provide the necessary defense was through taxing imported items.

A. How do American people pay for government?

  Ⓐ through debt
  Ⓑ through taxation
  Ⓒ through imported items
  Ⓓ through defense

 Clue Skim the passage then read the questions. You don't have to reread the story for each question.

● Practice

The Electoral College

    The electoral college was created by the Constitution because the Founding Fathers did not want the president elected by Congress or the people. It is a group of delegates chosen by the voters to elect the president and vice president. On Election Day, the first Tuesday after the first Monday in November, voters mark a ballot for president and vice president. They do not actually vote for the candidates, but they select electors, or delegates, to represent their state in the electoral college. Each state has as many votes in the electoral college as it has senators and representatives. There are 538 electors. The electors meet in December on a date set by law to cast their votes. The results are sent to the president of the Senate who opens them. A candidate must receive 270 or a majority of the electoral votes to win. After two representatives from each body of Congress have counted the electoral votes, the results are officially announced in January. The public knows the results right after the November election because the news media figures them out. These results are not official until Congress has counted the electoral votes. A candidate may win the popular vote but lose the election.

 GO ON

SOCIAL STUDIES

● Lesson 2: Reading and Understanding (cont.)

1. **The electoral college was created by the—**
   - (A) president.
   - (B) Constitution.
   - (C) Bill of Rights.
   - (D) delegates.

2. **When is Election Day?**
   - (F) the Thursday after the first Monday in November
   - (G) the Monday after the first Sunday in November
   - (H) the Tuesday after the last Friday in November
   - (J) the Tuesday after the first Monday in November

3. **Each state has as many votes in the electoral college as it has—**
   - (A) senators and representatives.
   - (B) senators and registered voters.
   - (C) representatives and registered voters.
   - (D) tax payers.

4. **There are how many electors?**
   - (F) 270
   - (G) 538
   - (H) 2 per state
   - (J) as many as needed

5. **What is required for a candidate to win?**
   - (A) delegates
   - (B) a majority of electoral votes
   - (C) electoral college
   - (D) representatives from each state

6. **A candidate may win the popular vote but lose the election. Explain why this does or does not seem fair to you.**

   _____

   _____

   _____

   _____

   _____

   _____

   _____

   _____

Name _____   Date_____

● Lesson 3: Reading and Understanding

Directions: Read the passages and select the best answer for each question.

Example

Amendments 13, 14, and 15 are often called the Civil Rights Amendments because they clarified the rights of slaves after the Civil War. The civil rights movement, which emerged in the 1950s and 1960s, helped make these principles a reality in America.	**A. Which amendments are often called the Civil Rights Amendments?** Ⓐ 13 and 15 Ⓑ 14, 15, and 16 Ⓒ 13, 14, and 15 Ⓓ 11, 12, and 13

 Skim the passage then read the questions. You don't have to reread the story for each question.

● Practice

Dictatorships and Democracies

A *dictatorship* occurs in a nation whose government is completely under the control of a dictator, or all-powerful ruler. The twentieth century saw the rise of many dictatorships. Near the end of World War I, Russia became a Communist dictatorship. In 1933 Adolf Hitler set up a dictatorship in Germany. Dictatorships were also set up in Italy, Spain, and most of the Balkan nations. Although dictatorships may have written constitutions and elections, the constitutions do not give freedom to their people, and the government controls the elections. In a dictatorship, people are not allowed to disagree with the government. The idea of individual rights is not valued in a dictatorship. Instead, individuals are valued only to the extent they can serve the government. Democracies are the opposite of dictatorships. Democratic government is considered to be the servant of the people, rather than the other way around. Democracies are based on the idea that the people rule. Authority to govern comes from the people. In a democracy, fair and free elections are held regularly. Without an informed and questioning citizenry, a democracy could not survive.

SOCIAL STUDIES

● **Lesson 3: Reading and Understanding (cont.)**

1. A nation that is under the control of an all-powerful ruler is called a(n)—
    - (A) democracy.
    - (B) dictatorship.
    - (C) communist.
    - (D) authoritarian.

2. Which century saw the rise of many dictatorships?
    - (F) nineteenth
    - (G) seventeenth
    - (H) eighteenth
    - (J) twentieth

3. Adolf Hitler set up a dictatorship in what country?
    - (A) Italy
    - (B) Spain
    - (C) Germany
    - (D) Russia

4. Who rules in a democracy?
    - (F) dictators
    - (G) government workers
    - (H) the people
    - (J) Democrats

5. In a dictatorship, who controls the elections?
    - (A) the government
    - (B) the president
    - (C) the voters
    - (D) informed citizenry

6. The idea of individual rights is not valued in a—
    - (F) democracy.
    - (G) dictatorship.
    - (H) election.
    - (J) free government.

STOP

Name _____   Date _____

SOCIAL STUDIES
SAMPLE TEST

● **Directions:** Read each question carefully. Select the correct answer.

Examples

A. The United States government was set up with three ruling branches of government based on—

- Ⓐ the early British parliament.
- Ⓑ the early Roman republic.
- Ⓒ the early Greek democracy.
- Ⓓ the early Roman dictatorship.

B. The Industrial Revolution is characterized by all of the following except—

- Ⓕ encouragement of invention.
- Ⓖ no one could get rich.
- Ⓗ growth of democracy.
- Ⓙ encouragement of literature and the arts.

---

1. The world volume of trade increased and the Atlantic Ocean replaced the Mediterranean Sea as the center of world trade during this expansion.

- Ⓐ American
- Ⓑ European
- Ⓒ Australian
- Ⓓ African

2. In Italy and Spain, the _____ tried to stop the spread of Protestantism during the 16th century.

- Ⓕ Puritans
- Ⓖ Kings
- Ⓗ Inquisition
- Ⓙ Lutherans

3. Ferdinand Magellan was a famous explorer from which country?

- Ⓐ Spain
- Ⓑ Italy
- Ⓒ England
- Ⓓ Holland

4. What is the definition of a <u>ziggurat</u>?

- Ⓕ a burial chamber in Egypt
- Ⓖ a mud-brick structure built at the center of a city-state in Mesopotamia
- Ⓗ a type of canal
- Ⓙ ancient housing

5. What was the effect of plants and animals becoming more plentiful during the Old Stone Age?

- Ⓐ There was a food shortage.
- Ⓑ The number of people on earth grew.
- Ⓒ Trade routes opened up.
- Ⓓ The earth quickly became overpopulated.

GO ON

SOCIAL STUDIES
SAMPLE TEST (cont.)

6. What does the term <u>land bridge</u> mean in the following sentence:

   One way people may have learned to survive was to migrate across a land bridge to other continents.

   (F) huge sheets of ice

   (G) land mass that connects two larger land masses

   (H) land that is surrounded by water on three sides

   (J) a bridge made by building an earthen passage over a river

7. Who was King Hammurabi?

   (A) a ruler of Babylon who wrote one of the world's oldest code of laws

   (B) a ruler of Rome who built aqueducts

   (C) a great Pharaoh of Egypt

   (D) a great king who built important trade routes

8. Which one of the following statements about archaeology is false?

   (F) The higher the B.C. date, the later that time is in history.

   (G) Fossils are the remains of plants and animals from the past.

   (H) Archaeologists use radiocarbon dating.

   (J) Archaeologists use grid squares to record the exact locations of objects.

9. The first system of writing that was developed in the Mesopotamian region of Sumer was called—

   (A) Latin.

   (B) manuscript.

   (C) hieroglyphics.

   (D) cuneiform.

10. The European Renaissance began where?

   (F) Spain

   (G) Britain

   (H) France

   (J) Italy

11. In ancient Egypt, important documents were written on <u>papyrus</u>. Write the following sentences in the correct order:

   The strips were laid across each other. Reeds from the Nile River were chopped. The sheets were hung up to dry. The inner part of the reeds was cut into strips. The strips were pounded with a mallet until they were "glued" together.

   _____

   _____

   _____

   _____

STOP

ANSWER SHEET

STUDENT'S NAME		SCHOOL

LAST   **FIRST**   **MI**

TEACHER

FEMALE ◯   MALE ◯

BIRTH DATE

MONTH	DAY	YEAR

JAN ◯
FEB ◯
MAR ◯
APR ◯
MAY ◯
JUN ◯
JUL ◯
AUG ◯
SEP ◯
OCT ◯
NOV ◯
DEC ◯

GRADE ⑥ ⑦ ⑧

SOCIAL STUDIES

A Ⓐ Ⓑ Ⓒ Ⓓ	**4** Ⓕ Ⓖ Ⓗ Ⓙ	**9** Ⓐ Ⓑ Ⓒ Ⓓ	**14** Ⓕ Ⓖ Ⓗ Ⓙ	**19** Ⓐ Ⓑ Ⓒ Ⓓ
B Ⓕ Ⓖ Ⓗ Ⓙ	**5** Ⓐ Ⓑ Ⓒ Ⓓ	**10** Ⓕ Ⓖ Ⓗ Ⓙ	**15** Ⓐ Ⓑ Ⓒ Ⓓ	**20** Ⓕ Ⓖ Ⓗ Ⓙ
1 Ⓐ Ⓑ Ⓒ Ⓓ	**6** Ⓕ Ⓖ Ⓗ Ⓙ	**11** Ⓐ Ⓑ Ⓒ Ⓓ	**16** Ⓕ Ⓖ Ⓗ Ⓙ	
2 Ⓕ Ⓖ Ⓗ Ⓙ	**7** Ⓐ Ⓑ Ⓒ Ⓓ	**12** Ⓕ Ⓖ Ⓗ Ⓙ	**17** Ⓐ Ⓑ Ⓒ Ⓓ	
3 Ⓐ Ⓑ Ⓒ Ⓓ	**8** Ⓕ Ⓖ Ⓗ Ⓙ	**13** Ⓐ Ⓑ Ⓒ Ⓓ	**18** Ⓕ Ⓖ Ⓗ Ⓙ	

Name _____ Date _____

SOCIAL STUDIES PRACTICE TEST

● **Directions:** Read each question carefully. Select the correct answer.

Examples

A. **In what era did people learn to make tools out of stone?**
- (A) Iron Age
- (B) Jurassic Era
- (C) Bronze Age
- (D) Old Stone Age

B. **What revolution was started in the middle of the 18th century and is characterized by an increase in the invention and use of machinery?**
- (F) French
- (G) American
- (H) Industrial
- (J) Machine

1. **Which group of early humans was the most advanced?**
- (A) Homo erectus
- (B) Homo habilis
- (C) Homo sapiens
- (D) Australopithecus

2. **Who heads the judicial branch of the United States?**
- (F) Supreme Court
- (G) House of Representatives
- (H) Senate
- (J) vice president

3. **What is Hippocrates often called?**
- (A) the "father of medicine"
- (B) the "father of Greece"
- (C) the "great teacher"
- (D) the "father of Greek architecture"

4. **A type of government in which a king rules over the citizens is called a—**
- (F) republic.
- (G) democracy.
- (H) dictatorship.
- (J) monarchy.

GO ON

SOCIAL STUDIES PRACTICE TEST

(cont.)

5. A **peninsula** is—
    - (A) a body of land between two rivers.
    - (B) an inlet from an ocean.
    - (C) land surrounded by water on three sides.
    - (D) water surrounded by mountains on three sides.

6. **Alexander became known as "Alexander the Great" because—**
    - (F) he tamed wild horses.
    - (G) he created a huge Greek empire.
    - (H) he was the son of the King of Macedonia.
    - (J) he was highly respected.

7. **A person who rules with total power is a—**
    - (A) republican.
    - (B) democrat.
    - (C) autocrat.
    - (D) dictator.

8. **When did the Roman Empire reach its greatest size?**
    - (F) about 1500 B.C.
    - (G) about A.D. 2000
    - (H) about A.D. 117
    - (J) about 4000 B.C.

9. **Which of the following describes the Hanging Gardens of Babylon?**
    - (A) It is made up of raised balconies.
    - (B) It is the oldest of the wonders.
    - (C) It is a 40-foot-high statue.
    - (D) It honored the sun god Helios.

10. **What do we call something that tries to explain why a prehistoric event happened or how something was created?**
    - (F) fantasy
    - (G) make believe
    - (H) gods and goddesses
    - (J) myth

11. **Which of the following was an important new source of power during the Industrial Revolution?**
    - (A) gasoline
    - (B) water
    - (C) steam
    - (D) nuclear

12. **Many inventions come from ancient China. Which one of the following did not?**
    - (F) seismograph
    - (G) paper
    - (H) phonograph
    - (J) compass

13. **Where did the first major Greek civilization begin?**
    - (A) Asia Minor
    - (B) Mount Olympus
    - (C) Rome
    - (D) Crete

GO ON

1-57768-977-1 — *Spectrum Test Practice 7*

SOCIAL STUDIES PRACTICE TEST
(cont.)

14. Confucius, a master teacher in China, taught, "If you make a mistake and do not correct it, this is called a mistake." What does this lesson mean?

  Ⓕ Correcting a mistake is the right thing to do.

  Ⓖ It is appropriate to not worry about correcting a mistake.

  Ⓗ It is sometimes fine to make mistakes.

  Ⓙ No mistake should be forgiven.

15. The "Silk Road" was a trade route that linked which of the following regions?

  Ⓐ China to Russia

  Ⓑ China to the Middle East and Europe

  Ⓒ China to South America

  Ⓓ China to Africa

16. The word *pyramid* comes from the Greek words *pyra*, meaning _____, and *midas*, meaning "measure".

  Ⓕ fire or light

  Ⓖ bowl

  Ⓗ pasta

  Ⓙ sand

17. A deposit of soil that accumulates at the mouth of a river is called a—

  Ⓐ dune.

  Ⓑ fiord.

  Ⓒ peninsula.

  Ⓓ delta.

18. All but which one of the following individuals was a famous Greek during the "Golden Age"?

  Ⓕ Pericles

  Ⓖ Hercules

  Ⓗ Socrates

  Ⓙ Hippocrates

19. Which of the following is not one of the three main time periods of Egypt?

  Ⓐ Old Kingdom

  Ⓑ Ancient Kingdom

  Ⓒ Middle Kingdom

  Ⓓ New Kingdom

20. What type of government is characterized by nobles ruling with the kings?

  Ⓕ oligarchy

  Ⓖ democracy

  Ⓗ federalist

  Ⓙ parliament

21. Write a paragraph describing a hardship you might have encountered if you had been a pioneer traveling on the Oregon Trail.

  _____

  _____

  _____

  _____

  _____

STOP

READING: VOCABULARY
Lesson 1: Synonyms
• Page 11
- A. C
- B. H
- 1. A
- 2. G
- 3. B
- 4. H
- 5. C
- 6. F
- 7. B
- 8. H

READING: VOCABULARY
Lesson 2: Antonyms
• Page 12
- A. A
- B. H
- 1. A
- 2. G
- 3. A
- 4. H
- 5. D
- 6. F
- 7. D
- 8. F

READING: VOCABULARY
Lesson 3: Multi-Meaning words
• Page 13
- A. D
- B. G
- 1. B
- 2. F
- 3. C
- 4. H
- 5. D
- 6. G
- 7. D

READING: VOCABULARY
Lesson 4: Words in Context
• Page 14
- A. A
- B. H
- 1. B
- 2. J
- 3. A
- 4. H
- 5. B
- 6. F

READING: VOCABULARY
SAMPLE TEST
• Pages 15–16
- A. D
- B. F
- 1. D
- 2. H
- 3. A
- 4. G
- 5. A
- 6. H
- 7. B
- 8. J
- 9. B
- 10. J
- 11. A
- 12. J
- 13. C
- 14. G

READING: READING COMPREHENSION
Lesson 5: Main Idea
• Page 17
- A. B
- 1. B
- 2. J

READING: READING COMPREHENSION
Lesson 6: Recalling Details
• Page 18
- A. A
- 1. B
- 2. J

READING: READING COMPREHENSION
Lesson 7: Inferencing
• Page 19
- A. C
- 1. D
- 2. F

READING: READING COMPREHENSION
Lesson 8: Fact and Opinion
• Page 20
- A. D
- 1. B
- 2. G

READING: READING COMPREHENSION
Lesson 9: Story Elements
• Page 21
- A. A
- 1. D
- 2. G

READING: READING COMPREHENSION
Lesson 10: Nonfiction
• Pages 22–23
- A. A
- 1. A
- 2. G
- 3. D
- 4. F
- 5. B
- 6. F

READING: READING COMPREHENSION
Lesson 11: Nonfiction
• Pages 24–25
- A. A
- 1. D
- 2. J
- 3. A
- 4. H
- 5. B
- 6. F

READING: READING COMPREHENSION
Lesson 12: Nonfiction
• Pages 26–27
- A. B
- 1. A
- 2. G
- 3. C
- 4. H
- 5. D
- 6. J

READING: READING COMPREHENSION
Lesson 13: Fiction
• Pages 28–29
- A. A
- 1. A
- 2. J
- 3. B
- 4. J
- 5. C
- 6. J

READING: READING COMPREHENSION
Lesson 14: Fiction
• Pages 30–31
- A. A
- 1. A
- 2. H
- 3. D
- 4. J
- 5. C
- 6. G

READING: READING COMPREHENSION
Lesson 15: Fiction
• Pages 32–33
- A. D
- 1. B
- 2. J
- 3. B
- 4. H
- 5. A
- 6. G

READING COMPREHENSION SAMPLE TEST
• Pages 34–35
- A. D
- 1. C
- 2. G
- 3. A
- 4. G
- 5. C
- 6. J

READING COMPREHENSION SAMPLE TEST
• Pages 36–37
- A. D
- 1. D
- 2. H
- 3. C
- 4. F
- 5. B
- 6. H

READING: PRACTICE TEST
Part 1: Vocabulary
• Page 39
- A. A
- B. G
- 1. B
- 2. H
- 3. B
- 4. F
- 5. C
- 6. F
- 7. B
- 8. H

READING: PRACTICE TEST
Part 1: Vocabulary

• Page 40
9. A
10. H
11. B
12. G
13. A
14. H
15. C
16. J
17. B
18. H

READING: PRACTICE TEST
Part 1: Vocabulary
• Page 41
19. B
20. G
21. B
22. F
23. D
24. F
25. B
26. F
27. C
28. G

READING: PRACTICE TEST
Part 1: Vocabulary
• Page 42
29. A
30. G
31. B
32. J
33. C
34. F
35. A
36. H
37. A
38. H

READING: PRACTICE TEST
Part 2: Reading Comprehension
• Pages 43–44
A. C
1. C
2. H
3. C
4. G
5. C
6. J

READING: PRACTICE TEST
Part 2: Reading Comprehension
• Pages 45–46
A. D
7. C
8. G
9. B
10. G
11. B
12. H

LANGUAGE MECHANICS
Lesson 1: Punctuation
• Pages 47–48
A. C
B. G
1. C
2. G
3. B
4. G
5. A
6. J

7. D
8. F
9. A
10. G
11. B
12. J
13. D
14. H

LANGUAGE: LANGUAGE MECHANICS
Lesson 2: Capitalization and Punctuation
• Pages 49–50
A. B
B. J
1. A
2. G
3. A
4. H
5. A
6. G
7. C
8. H
9. C
10. F
11. A
12. G
13. A
14. F

LANGUAGE MECHANICS SAMPLE TEST
• Pages 51–53
A. C
B. J
1. C
2. J
3. A
4. G
5. C
6. G
7. B
8. J
9. D
10. F
11. D
12. H
13. D
14. F
15. A
16. H
17. C
18. J
19. B
20. G
21. A
22. G

LANGUAGE: LANGUAGE EXPRESSION
Lesson 3: Usage
• Pages 54–56
A. B
B. F
1. C
2. F
3. A
4. J
5. B
6. H

7. D
8. H
9. A
10. J
11. C
12. J
13. A
14. J
15. A
16. J
17. C
18. F
19. C

LANGUAGE: LANGUAGE EXPRESSION
Lesson 4: Sentences
• Pages 57–59
A. B
B. J
1. B
2. H
3. B
4. G
5. C
6. G
7. A
8. J
9. B
10. H
11. A
12. J
13. C
14. J

LANGUAGE: LANGUAGE EXPRESSION
Lesson 5: Paragraphs
• Pages 60–62
A. A
1. B
2. F
3. B
4. H
5. D
6. H
7. B
8. F
9. A
10. F

LANGUAGE: LANGUAGE EXPRESSION SAMPLE TEST
• Pages 63–67
A. D
B. F
1. C
2. J
3. A
4. H
5. A
6. J
7. B
8. J
9. A
10. J
11. B
12. J
13. B
14. F
15. D

16. J
17. C
18. F
19. C
20. G
21. C
22. G
23. D
24. J
25. A
26. H
27. C
28. J
29. C
30. F
31. D

LANGUAGE: SPELLING
Lesson 6: Spelling
• Pages 68–69
A. B
B. H
1. D
2. F
3. A
4. H
5. A
6. G
7. D
8. G
9. A
10. J
11. B
12. F
13. C
14. H

LANGUAGE: SPELLING SAMPLE TEST
• Pages 70–71
A. C
B. G
1. A
2. H
3. D
4. F
5. C
6. J
7. C
8. F
9. C
10. G
11. D
12. F
13. B
14. J

LANGUAGE: STUDY SKILLS
Lesson 7: Study Skills
• Pages 72–74
A. A
B. H
1. A
2. H
3. D
4. F
5. A
6. G
7. D
8. H
9. B

10. J
11. A
12. J
13. B
14. H

LANGUAGE: STUDY SKILLS SAMPLE TEST
• Pages 75–76
A. C
B. H
1. A
2. G
3. D
4. G
5. C
6. F
7. C
8. G
9. D
10. F
11. A

LANGUAGE PRACTICE TEST
Part1: Language Mechanics
• Pages 78–79
A. A
B. G
1. C
2. J
3. A
4. H
5. A
6. J
7. C
8. J
9. A
10. H
11. A
12. G
13. D
14. G
15. A

LANGUAGE PRACTICE TEST
Part 2: Language Expression
• Pages 80–83
A. A
B. J
1. A
2. H
3. B
4. F
5. C
6. J
7. B
8. H
9. D
10. J
11. B
12. F
13. C
14. H
15. A
16. J
17. C
18. G
19. A
20. H
21. D
22. J

23. C
24. F
25. D

LANGUAGE PRACTICE TEST
Part 3: Spelling
• Pages 84–85
A. B
B. H
1. A
2. J
3. B
4. H
5. B
6. F
7. C
8. J
9. A
10. F
11. D
12. J
13. B
14. H

LANGUAGE PRACTICE TEST
Part 4: Study Skills
• Pages 86–87
A. C
B. F
1. A
2. H
3. D
4. H
5. C
6. H
7. D
8. J
9. B
10. J
11. B

MATH: MATH CONCEPTS
Lesson 1: Numeration
• Pages 88–90
A. B
B. H
1. C
2. G
3. D
4. F
5. B
6. G
7. C
8. J
9. C
10. G
11. A
12. G
13. D
14. J
15. D
16. F
17. D
18. G
19. C

MATH: MATH CONCEPTS
Lesson 2: Number Concepts
• Pages 91–93
A. A
B. J
1. B
2. G
3. A
4. J
5. B
6. G
7. D
8. H
9. C
10. H
11. A
12. J
13. A
14. H
15. D
16. H
17. B
18. F
19. D
20. H

MATH: MATH CONCEPTS
Lesson 3: Fractions and Decimals
• Pages 94–96
A. A
1. C
2. H
3. B
4. F
5. D
6. F
7. B
8. F
9. C
10. G
11. D
12. F
13. C
14. J
15. A
16. J
17. A
18. G

MATH: MATH CONCEPTS
SAMPLE TEST
• Pages 97–99
A. D
B. H
1. B
2. F
3. D
4. F
5. B
6. J
7. A
8. G
9. B
10. J
11. B
12. H
13. D
14. H
15. B
16. F

17. D
18. H
19. A
20. H
21. A

MATH: COMPUTATION
Lesson 4: Fractions, Addition and Subtraction
• Page 100
A. C
B. F
1. A
2. J
3. A
4. G
5. C
6. J

MATH: COMPUTATION
Lesson 5: Fractions, Multiplication and Division
• Page 101
A. B
B. F
1. A
2. J
3. A
4. H
5. A
6. G

MATH: COMPUTATION
Lesson 6: Decimals, Addition and Subtraction
• Page 102
A. B
B. G
1. D
2. F
3. C
4. F
5. A
6. H

MATH: COMPUTATION
Lesson 7: Decimals, Multiplication and Division
• Page 103
A. B
B. F
1. A
2. J
3. A
4. J
5. B
6. H

MATH: COMPUTATION
Lesson 8: Percents, Converting to Decimals
• Page 104
A. C
B. G
1. C
2. J
3. B
4. F
5. D
6. H

MATH: COMPUTATION
Lesson 9: Percents, Finding Percentages of a Number
• Page 105
A. D
B. F
1. B
2. G
3. C
4. J
5. A
6. H

MATH: COMPUTATION
Lesson 10: Problem Solving, Addition and Subtraction
• Page 106
A. D
B. F
1. B
2. F
3. C
4. J

MATH: COMPUTATION
Lesson 11: Problem Solving, Multiplication and Division
• Page 107
A. C
B. G
1. C
2. F
3. A
4. J

MATH: COMPUTATION
SAMPLE TEST
• Pages 108–110
A. A
B. G
1. C
2. J
3. A
4. G
5. D
6. F
7. A
8. J
9. A
10. G
11. A
12. H
13. D
14. G
15. B
16. H
17. D
18. F
19. D
20. G
21. C
22. H
23. A
24. G

MATH: APPLICATIONS
Lesson 12: Geometry
• Pages 111–113
A. C
B. H
1. D
2. G

ANSWER KEY

3. A
4. H
5. D
6. G
7. A
8. H
9. C
10. H
11. A
12. H
13. D
14. H
15. A
16. G
17. B
18. F

MATH APPLICATIONS
Lesson 13: Measurement
• Pages 114–115
A. B
B. H
1. A
2. J
3. C
4. G
5. D
6. F
7. C
8. G
9. C
10. F
11. D
12. G

MATH: APPLICATION
Lesson 14: Problem Solving
• Pages 116–118
A. D
B. H
1. A
2. H
3. B
4. H
5. B
6. F
7. D
8. H
9. C
10. J
11. D
12. G
13. D
14. G
15. A
16. F
17. C
18. H

MATH: APPLICATIONS
Lesson 15: Algebra
• Pages 119–120
A. D
B. F
1. B
2. H
3. D
4. F
5. A
6. J
7. A

8. G
9. D
10. H
11. C
12. G

MATH APPLICATIONS
SAMPLE TEST
• Pages 121–124
A. B
B. G
1. B
2. H
3. B
4. F
5. C
6. J
7. A
8. J
9. C
10. F
11. A
12. G
13. C
14. F
15. C
16. G
17. C
18. F

MATH PRACTICE TEST
Part 1: Concepts
• Pages 125–126
A. C
B. G
1. A
2. G
3. C
4. G
5. C
6. F
7. A
8. G
9. A
10. J
11. D
12. F
13. B
14. J

MATH PRACTICE TEST
Part 2: Computation
• Pages 127–128
A. B
B. F
1. C
2. J
3. A
4. J
5. C
6. G
7. A
8. J
9. A
10. H
11. B
12. H
13. A
14. F
15. D
16. J

17. A
18. G

MATH PRACTICE TEST
Lesson 3: Applications
• Pages 129–130
A. C
B. G
1. A
2. H
3. A
4. J
5. D
6. J
7. A
8. J
9. A
10. F
11. A
12. H
13. D
14. F

SCIENCE
Lesson 1: General Knowledge
• Pages 131–133
A. A
B. G
1. C
2. H
3. C
4. F
5. A
6. G
7. D
8. J
9. B
10. F
11. D
12. H
13. D
14. H
15. D
16. F

SCIENCE
Lesson 2: Reading and Understanding
• Pages 134–136
A. A
1. D
2. G
3. B
4. Answers will vary.
5. D
6. B
7. H
8. D
9. Answers will vary.
10. A
11. C
12. F
13. D
14. G

SCIENCE SAMPLE TEST
• Pages 137–138
A. C
B. H
1. A
2. J
3. D

4. F
5. B
6. G
7. C
8. H
9. D
10. F
11. Answers will vary.

SCIENCE PRACTICE TEST
• Pages 140–141

A. B
B. G
1. C
2. H
3. A
4. G
5. D
6. G
7. A
8. J
9. D
10. H
11. Air molecules move faster in warm air, therefore, bumping into one another more frequently.

SOCIAL STUDIES
Lesson 1: General Knowledge
• Pages 142–144

A. B
B. H
1. C
2. G
3. A
4. J
5. D
6. G
7. C
8. F
9. A
10. H
11. A
12. H
13. B
14. H
15. D
16. H
17. Answers will vary.

SOCIAL STUDIES
Lesson 2: Reading and Understanding
• Pages 145–146

A. B
1. B
2. J
3. A
4. G
5. B
6. Answers will vary.

SOCIAL STUDIES
Lesson 2: Reading and Understanding
• Pages 147–148

A. C
1. B
2. J
3. C
4. H

5. A
6. G

SOCIAL STUDIES
SAMPLE TEST
• Pages 149–150

A. B
B. G
1. B
2. H
3. A
4. G
5. B
6. G
7. A
8. F
9. D
10. J
11. 1. Reeds from the Nile were chopped. 2. The inner part of the reeds was cut into strips. 3. The strips were laid across each other. 4. The strips were pounded with a mallet until they were "glued" together. 5. The sheets were hung up to dry.

SOCIAL STUDIES PRACTICE TEST
• Pages 152–154

A. D
B. H
1. C
2. F
3. A
4. J
5. C
6. G
7. D
8. H
9. A
10. J
11. C
12. H
13. D
14. F
15. B
16. F
17. D
18. G
19. B
20. F
21. Answers will vary.